Better Homes and Gardens®

Best
Bread
MACHINE RECIPES

Better Homes and Gardens® Books
Des Moines, Iowa

Better Homes and Gardens® Books
An imprint of Meredith® Books

Best Bread Machine Recipes
Editor: Jennifer Darling
Contributing Editors: Spectrum Communication Services, Inc.
Associate Art Director: Tom Wegner
Copy Chief: Angela K. Renkoski
Copy Editor: Diane Nelson
Test Kitchen Director: Sharon Stilwell
Test Kitchen Product Supervisor: Marilyn Cornelius
Photographer: Andy Lyons
Food Stylist: Dianna Nolin
Photo Stylist: Gayle Schadendorf
Electronic Production Coordinator: Paula Forest
Editorial and Design Assistants: Judy Bailey, Jennifer Norris, Karen Schirm
Production Manager: Douglas M. Johnston
Prepress Coordinator: Marjorie J. Schenkelberg

Meredith® Books
Editor in Chief: James D. Blume
Managing Editor: Christopher Cavanaugh
Director, New Product Development: Ray Wolf
Vice President, General Manager: Jamie L. Martin

Better Homes and Gardens® **Magazine**
Editor in Chief: Jean LemMon
Executive Food Editor: Nancy Byal

Meredith Publishing Group
President, Publishing Group: Christopher M. Little
Vice President and Publishing Director: John P. Loughlin

Meredith Corporation
Chairman and Chief Executive Officer: Jack D. Rehm
President and Chief Operating Officer: William T. Kerr
Chairman of the Executive Committee: E.T. Meredith III

On the cover and page 4: Honey Grain Bread, page 41
On page 1: Wheat Cloverleaf Rolls, page 104, and Pine Nut Rolls, page 102

Our seal assures you that every recipe in *Best Bread Machine Recipes* has been tested in the Better Homes and Gardens® Test Kitchen. This means that each recipe is practical and reliable, and meets our high standards of taste appeal. We guarantee your satisfaction with this book for as long as you own it.

First Edition. Printing Number and Year: 10 9   02 01 00 99
Library of Congress Catalog Card Number: 96-78799
ISBN: 0-696-20682-X

CONTENTS

*O*ne of the handiest and most versatile tools in your kitchen is also the easiest to use. The bread machine, that marvel of baking power, expands your baking potential merely by sitting on the counter.

This recipe collection is designed to help you make the most of your bread machine—and have fun with it, too. Going far beyond the common loaves for toast and sandwiches, the 80 recipes in this book explore the endless possibilities of your machine, whether you turn bread dough into a main-dish pizza or a tempting dessert.

It all begins with our primer. This reference section covers all of the basics, including measuring and adding ingredients, checking dough consistency, and storing bread. In addition, the primer offers full instructions for converting your favorite recipes to work in the machine, plus answers to common bread-baking questions.

The eight recipe chapters cover a host of creative bread-baking options, from focaccia to coffee cakes and tea rings. The recipes work in any bread machine that makes a 1½- or 2-pound loaf, and some combine the machine's capabilities with other cooking techniques. For instance, several of the sweet treats in this book start out with dough mixed in the bread machine that is then shaped in a ring or twist and baked conventionally.

Throughout the book, you'll find handy tips and shortcuts to help you fit baking into your busy schedule. Best of all, you can bake these recipes with confidence, because each was tested for quality in the Better Homes and Gardens® Test Kitchen.

Can you live by bread alone? Maybe not, but when you team your bread machine with the creative, delicious recipes in this book, the thought becomes imminently appealing.

BREAD MACHINE PRIMER

*B*read machine manufacturers strive to make their products unique. Because of the many differences in machines, it's important that you get to know the features of your particular model. Then take a few minutes to review the following general guidelines.

KNOWING YOUR MACHINE

Different brands of machines vary when it comes to cycles, baking times, and temperatures. Here is a listing of several common cycles and settings to compare with the ones listed in your owner's manual.

Basic White: This all-purpose setting is used for most breads.

Whole Grain: This cycle provides the longer rising times needed for heavier breads that use whole wheat or rye flour or other varieties of whole grains.

Dough: This cycle mixes and kneads the bread dough and usually allows it to rise once before the cycle is complete. After this point, remove the dough for shaping, rising, and baking in your conventional oven.

Raisin: Some machines have a separate cycle with a signal about 5 minutes prior to the end of the second kneading cycle. This signal indicates that raisins, nuts, or other similar ingredients can be added. If your machine has no signal, try adding these ingredients about 25 minutes into the kneading cycle.

Sweet: The amount of sugar in a bread recipe affects its rising time and baking temperature. Some machines include this cycle for breads that have a high proportion of sugar. Follow the manufacturer's directions for when to use this cycle. If you find that bread baked on this cycle has gummy spots, try baking the bread on the basic white cycle.

Rapid: Some machines offer a cycle that reduces the total time needed for the machine to mix, rise, and bake a loaf of bread. Follow the manufacturer's directions to determine when to use this cycle.

Timed-Bake: This cycle allows ingredients to be added to the machine at one time and the processing to begin at a later time. Do not use the timed-bake cycle with recipes that include fresh milk, eggs, cheese, and other perishable foods. Allowing these ingredients to stand at room temperature for long periods will cause them to spoil. (See the chart on page 8 to substitute dry milk powder for fresh milk.)

Crust Color Setting: This setting lets you choose the baking time to control the brownness of the crust. For most breads, the best choice is the medium setting. If you find that your machine browns breads excessively, try a light-crust setting. Recipes that are high in sugar also may benefit from a lighter setting. However, with a lighter setting, the bread may be slightly gummy.

CHOOSING YOUR RECIPE

For best results, always read a recipe completely before you start to make sure you understand it and have all the ingredients on hand. The recipes in this book list ingredients for both 1½- and 2-pound loaves so you can select the appropriate size to fit your needs and your machine. For the most part, recipe directions apply to both sizes. Occasionally, however, there are special directions for the 2-pound recipe.

You'll find that a number of recipes throughout the book include this note: "For the 1½-pound loaf, the bread machine pan must have a capacity of 10 cups or more. For the 2-pound loaf, the bread machine must have a capacity of 12 cups or more."

Check your owner's manual to see if it lists your machine's pan capacity. If it doesn't, you'll need to measure the capacity of your pan. Here's how: Remove the pan from the bread machine. If necessary, tightly plug the hole for the paddle with crumpled foil. Use a liquid measuring cup to fill the pan with water until it is full to the brim, keeping track of the total amount of water added to the pan. For future reference, write the pan capacity in your owner's manual.

QUALITY RECIPES GUARANTEED

Each recipe in this book was tested by one of 10 experienced home economists in the Better Homes and Gardens® Test Kitchen. Recipes are judged on ease of preparation, texture, appeal, and flavor. No recipe can receive the Test Kitchen Seal of Approval until it meets the Test Kitchen's high standards. To ensure success, the recipes were tested in different machines from a variety of manufacturers including Black and Decker, Hitachi, Mr. Coffee, Mr. Loaf, Oster, Panasonic, Regal, Sanyo, Singer, Trillium, Toastmaster, West Bend, and Zojirushi.

INGREDIENT TIPS AND SUBSTITUTIONS

- All the recipes for loaves in this book call for between 1 and $1\frac{1}{2}$ teaspoons of active dry yeast or bread machine yeast. You may notice that this is less yeast than is used in many recipes supplied by bread machine manufacturers. In our testing, we found this amount of yeast makes a nicely risen loaf with an attractive shape. Adding more yeast typically produces a loaf with a very coarse and/or uneven texture. Also, it may cause the dough to rise too high then fall or stick to the lid of your machine or run over the edges of the pan.
- Use the following equivalents to substitute dry milk powder for fresh milk.

Fresh Milk	=	Dry Milk Powder	+	Water
$\frac{1}{2}$ cup		2 tablespoons		$\frac{1}{2}$ cup
$\frac{2}{3}$ cup		2 tablespoons		$\frac{2}{3}$ cup
$\frac{3}{4}$ cup		3 tablespoons		$\frac{3}{4}$ cup
1 cup		$\frac{1}{4}$ cup		1 cup
$1\frac{1}{4}$ cups		$\frac{1}{3}$ cup		$1\frac{1}{4}$ cups
$1\frac{1}{3}$ cups		$\frac{1}{3}$ cup + 1 tablespoon		$1\frac{1}{4}$ cups
$1\frac{1}{2}$ cups		$\frac{1}{2}$ cup		$1\frac{1}{3}$ cups

- Sour milk is a good substitute for buttermilk. To make 1 cup sour milk, add 1 tablespoon vinegar or lemon juice to a 1-cup liquid measuring cup, then add enough low-fat milk to measure 1 cup liquid. Dry buttermilk powder is also available.
- Refrigerated or thawed frozen egg product can be used in place of whole eggs (1 egg equals $\frac{1}{4}$ cup egg product). Egg whites also can be used instead of whole eggs (2 egg whites equal 1 whole egg).

• For best results when using margarine, choose a margarine or a stick spread that contains at least 60 percent vegetable oil. Do not use an "extra light" spread that contains only about 40 percent vegetable oil.

• When you are using more than 2 tablespoons of either margarine or butter, cut it into small pieces to ensure that it properly blends with the other ingredients.

MEASURING INGREDIENTS

Measuring accurately is crucial when baking. Incorrect proportions of liquid to dry ingredients may cause the recipe to fail. To avoid problems, follow these suggestions:

Flour. Stir the flour to lighten it before measuring and use metal or plastic measuring cups designed for dry ingredients. Gently spoon the flour into the cup and level off the top with the straight edge of a knife or metal spatula.

Liquid Ingredients. Use a glass or clear plastic measuring cup for liquids. Place the cup on a level surface and bend down so your eye is level with the marking you wish to read. Fill the cup to the marking. Don't lift the cup off the counter to your eye—it's impossible to hold the cup steady enough for an accurate reading. When using a measuring spoon to measure a liquid, pour the liquid just to the top of the spoon without letting it spill over. Don't hold the spoon over the machine pan while adding the liquid because the liquid could overflow from the spoon into the pan.

Margarine or Butter. For premeasured sticks, use a sharp knife to cut off the amount needed, following the guidelines on the wrapper. (Use one ¼-pound stick for ½ cup or half of a stick for ¼ cup.) For butter that's not in premeasured sticks, soften it and measure as directed for shortening.

Shortening. Using a rubber spatula, press the shortening firmly into a measuring cup designed for dry ingredients or into a measuring spoon. Level it off with the straight edge of a knife or metal spatula.

Sugar. Press brown sugar firmly into a measuring cup designed for dry ingredients. The sugar should hold the shape of the cup when turned out. For measuring spoons, the sugar does not have to be packed. To measure granulated sugar, spoon the sugar into the measuring cup or spoon, then level it off with the straight edge of a knife or metal spatula.

CHECKING DOUGH CONSISTENCY

Because the kneading action of different bread machines varies, it's important to check the consistency of bread dough after the first 3 to 5 minutes of kneading.

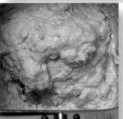

If the dough looks dry and crumbly (see photo, top left) or forms two or more balls, add additional liquid, 1 teaspoon at a time, until one smooth ball forms.

If the dough has too much moisture and does not form into a ball (see photo, center left), add additional bread flour, 1 tablespoon at a time, until a ball does form.

Bread dough with the correct amount of flour and liquid will form a smooth ball (see photo, left).

ADDING INGREDIENTS TO YOUR MACHINE

It's important to add ingredients to your machine according to the directions given in the owner's manual. Generally, manufacturers recommend adding the liquids first, followed by dry ingredients, with the yeast going in last. The reason for this is to keep the yeast away from the liquid ingredients until kneading begins. This is the order used for the recipes in this book.

RAISING DOUGH

When using the dough cycle, you often need to let the shaped dough rise before baking. For the best results, our Test Kitchen suggests using a warm, draft-free area where the temperature is between 80° and 85°.

An unheated oven is an ideal place for raising dough. Place the oven's lower rack in the lowest position; set a large pan of hot water on the rack. Cover the shaped dough loosely with a clean cloth and place it on the top rack of the oven. Close the door and let the dough rise until nearly doubled, using the time suggested in the recipe as a guide. Remove the dough and the water and preheat the oven.

However, it may not be the order the manufacturer recommends for your specific machine.

Also in this book, any ingredients listed after the yeast, such as dried fruits or nuts, should be added at the raisin bread cycle, if your machine has one. If not, add them according to the manufacturer's directions.

STORING BAKED AND UNBAKED BREAD

Remove hot bread from the machine as soon as it is done and place it on a wire rack to cool completely. (If the bread cools in the machine, it may become damp and soggy on the outside.)

● *To store at room temperature,* wrap the cooled bread in foil or plastic wrap, or place it in a plastic bag. Store it in a cool, dry place for up to 3 days.

● *To freeze,* place cooled bread in a freezer bag or container. Freeze the loaf for up to 3 months. To serve the frozen bread, thaw it in the packaging for 1 hour. Or, wrap the frozen bread in foil and thaw it in a 300° oven for about 20 minutes.

You can tailor recipes that use the bread machine's dough cycle to fit your schedule. Just make the dough as directed, refrigerate or freeze it, then shape and bake it later.

● *To refrigerate bread dough,* place it in an airtight container and refrigerate it for up to 24 hours. Bring the dough to room temperature before shaping it.

● *To freeze bread dough,* place it in an airtight container. Seal, label, and freeze for up to 3 months. To use the dough, let it stand at room temperature for 3 hours or until thawed. Or, thaw it overnight in the refrigerator. Shape and bake the bread as directed in the recipe.

HIGH-ALTITUDE TIPS

If you live in an area that is more than 1,000 feet above sea level, you'll need to make some adjustments to our bread machine recipes because of the lower atmospheric pressure. First, check your owner's manual for specific high-altitude directions. If none are given, start by reducing the yeast by $\frac{1}{4}$ teaspoon. At higher altitudes, breads will rise higher than at sea level and need less yeast. If your bread still rises too high, reduce the yeast by another $\frac{1}{4}$ teaspoon the next time you make the recipe.

Also, keep in mind that flour tends to be drier at high altitudes and sometimes will absorb more liquid. Watch the dough carefully as it mixes in the machine. If the dough seems dry, add additional liquid, 1 teaspoon at a time. Keep a record of the total amount of liquid you use as a reference for the next time you make the bread.

POINTERS FROM OUR TEST KITCHEN

Our Test Kitchen home economists have tested more than 3,000 bread machine recipes. Here are some valuable suggestions they have for making use of your bread machine as easy and reliable as possible.

• Use bread flour for each of the recipes in this book unless specified otherwise. This high-protein flour is especially formulated for bread baking.

• If you store flour or specialty grains in the freezer, warm the measured amount to room temperature before adding.

• Adding gluten flour to a bread that contains whole grain flour, especially rye flour, improves the texture of the loaf. (See gluten flour in glossary, page 13.)

• Salt is necessary when making yeast bread because it controls the growth of the yeast, which aids the rising of the dough. If you are on a sodium-restricted diet, you'll find most of the recipes in this book are lower in sodium than purchased breads. If you want breads even lower in sodium, experiment by reducing the salt in a recipe a little at a time.

• Yeast feeds on the sugar in bread dough, producing carbon dioxide gas that makes the dough rise. Either active dry yeast or bread machine yeast can be used in the recipes in this book. Store packages of dry yeast in a cool, dry place, and the yeast will stay fresh until the expiration date stamped on the package. Store an open jar of yeast tightly covered in the refrigerator. Use it before the expiration date printed on the jar. When baking bread at high altitudes, it may be necessary to reduce the amount of yeast in the recipe. (See "High Altitude Tips," page 11.)

• Make cleanup easy by spraying the kneading paddle of your machine with nonstick spray coating before adding the ingredients.

• If the kneading paddle stays in the bread when you remove the hot loaf from the machine, use the handle of a wooden spoon to help remove it.

• Fill the machine's pan with hot soapy water immediately after removing the baked bread. (Do not immerse the pan in water.) Soak the kneading paddle separately if it comes out with the loaf of bread.

SPECIALTY INGREDIENTS GLOSSARY

Barley is a cereal grain with a mild, starchy flavor and a slightly chewy texture. Pearl barley, the most popular form used for cooking, has the outer hull removed and has been polished or "pearled." It is sold in regular and quick-cooking forms. Store barley in an airtight container in a cool, dry place for up to 1 year.

Bread flour is a wheat flour made from hard wheat and has a higher protein and gluten content than all-purpose flour. Gluten provides structure and height to breads, making bread flour well-suited for the task. Store bread flour in an airtight container in a cool, dry place for up to 5 months or freeze it for up to 1 year.

Bulgur is a parched, cracked wheat product. To make it, the whole wheat kernels are soaked, cooked, and dried. Then some of the bran is removed and what remains of the kernels is cracked into small pieces. Bulgur has a delicate, nutty flavor. Store it in an airtight container in a cool, dry place for up to 6 months or freeze it for up to 1 year.

Cornmeal is made from dried yellow, white, or blue corn kernels that have been finely ground. Cornmeal labeled "stone ground" is slightly coarser than other cornmeals. Store cornmeal in an airtight container in a cool, dry place for up to 6 months or freeze it for up to 1 year.

Gluten flour, sometimes called wheat gluten, is made by removing most of the starch from high-protein, hard-wheat flour. If you can't find gluten flour at your supermarket, look for it at a health-food store. Store it in an airtight container in a cool, dry place for up to 5 months or freeze it for up to 1 year.

Millet is a cereal grain with tiny, round, yellow kernels that taste slightly nutty and have a chewy texture. Store millet in an airtight container in a cool, dry place for up to 2 years.

Oats are the cereal grain produced by the cereal grass of the same name. Oats have a nutty flavor and a chewy texture. Whole oats minus the hulls are called groats. Old-fashioned rolled oats are oat groats that have been steamed then flattened by steel rollers. Quick-cooking rolled oats are oat groats that are cut into small pieces—to shorten the cooking time—then flattened. Store oats in an airtight container in a cool, dry place for up to 6 months or freeze them for up to 1 year. *continued*

Rye flour is finely ground from rye, a cereal grain with dark brown kernels and a distinctive robust flavor. Light rye flour is sifted and contains less bran than dark rye flour. Store rye flour in an airtight container in a cool, dry place up to 5 months or freeze for up to 1 year.

Wheat germ is the embryo or sprouting section of the wheat kernel. It is sold both raw and toasted. Wheat germ is extremely perishable. Once opened, store it in the refrigerator for no more than 3 months.

Whole wheat flour, unlike all-purpose and bread flour, is ground from the complete wheat berry and contains the wheat germ as well as the wheat bran. It is coarser in texture and does not rise as well as all-purpose or bread flour. Store whole wheat flour in an airtight container in a cool, dry place for up to 5 months or freeze it for up to 1 year.

Wild rice is the long, dark brown or black, nutty-flavored seed of an annual marsh grass. It actually is not rice but a cereal grain. Store uncooked wild rice indefinitely in a cool, dry place or in the refrigerator.

"WHAT WENT WRONG?"

The following are some of the most commonly asked questions received by our Test Kitchen. If you run into a snag, the answers may help you avoid a problem the next time.

Q. Why is my loaf of bread small and heavy?

A. A short, compact loaf usually means the dough has not risen enough. The next time you make the recipe, check your measurements carefully. The ratio of flour to liquid has to be exact, and a little extra flour or liquid can throw the balance off. Also, make sure the yeast you're using is fresh. Be sure to use the yeast before the expiration date printed on the package or jar. In addition, always check the dough consistency as the bread kneads. You may need to add a little more liquid. (See "Checking Dough Consistency," page 10.)

Q. How can I make sure my bread isn't gummy?

A. Breads are usually gummy because they're underbaked. There are several reasons loaves don't bake completely. If the recipe is too large for the pan of your machine, the heat will not penetrate to the center of the loaf. Also, if you use the incorrect cycle or crust color setting, the bread will be underdone. Double-check your owner's manual to make sure you're using the correct settings. On some machines, the light color setting is too short to completely bake through some rich breads, so you may need to experiment to see what works for your machine.

Q. My bread collapsed. What happened?

A. Breads can collapse if they're too large for the pan or if the ratio of liquid to dry ingredients is not balanced. Make sure you are using a recipe that fits the capacity of your machine (see "Choosing Your Recipe," page 7) and that you are measuring the ingredients carefully. Also, loaves can fall if you've added too much yeast or if an ingredient, especially salt, is omitted. In addition, always check the dough consistency as the bread kneads. You may need to add a little more flour. (See "Checking Dough Consistency," page 10.) Weather also can affect bread baking. If the weather is warm and there is a lot of humidity, the dough may rise too fast, then collapse before baking begins.

Q. How can I avoid breads that look like mushrooms?

A. The main reason for mushroomed bread is that the recipe is too large for the pan of your machine. Check to confirm that your machine can accommodate the size loaf you're trying to make. (See "Choosing Your Recipe," page 7.) Check your measurements carefully, too. If the balance between liquid and dry ingredients is not correct, the bread may bake into a mushroom shape. Also, if the weather is quite warm, be sure to bake during the coolest part of the day, use refrigerated liquids, and try using the rapid cycle if your machine has one.

Q. My bread is very open-textured with many holes. How can I make a finer, more even-textured bread?

A. Breads can have a coarse texture or lots of air pockets for several reasons. First, if the ingredients aren't measured accurately, you may have added too much yeast, or the proportion of liquid to dry ingredients may be off, causing an open texture. Second, omitting the salt will result in a coarse bread. Third, check the dough consistency as the bread kneads. You may need to add a little more flour. (See "Checking Dough Consistency," page 10.) Finally, warm weather and high humidity can cause the yeast to rise too fast resulting in numerous large holes.   *continued*

Q. My loaf has a bumpy, uneven top and a very dense texture. How can I bake a nice rounded loaf?

A. When your bread turns out heavy with an uneven top, check your flour. Make sure it's fresh. If it has been stored a long time, it may be dried out and will not have the correct moisture content. (If you live at a high altitude, see "High-Altitude Tips," page 11.) Also, measure carefully. If you don't include the right amount of the liquid ingredients, or use too much flour, the loaf often bakes with a bumpy surface. Finally, always check the dough consistency as the bread kneads. You may need to add a little more liquid. (See "Checking Dough Consistency," page 10.)

CONVERTING YOUR FAVORITE RECIPES

If you have some prized bread recipes that you'd like to make in your bread machine, read on. And remember, the first time you try a new bread in your machine, watch and listen carefully. You may have to make adjustments, and it often takes more than one attempt before the bread turns out the way you like it.

Manufacturers sometimes include tips in their owner's manuals for converting traditional bread recipes to their particular bread machines. Before reading the information at right, review your manual for any hints that apply to your machine.

- Reduce the yeast to 1 teaspoon for a 1½-pound machine or 1¼ teaspoons for a 2-pound machine.
- Reduce the amount of flour to 3 cups for a 1½-pound machine or 4 cups for a 2-pound machine.
- Reduce all other ingredients by the same proportion as you reduce the flour. If a range is given for the flour, use the lower amount to figure the reduction proportion. For example, for a 1½-pound bread machine, a recipe calling for 1 package of yeast and 4½ cups flour would be decreased to use 1 teaspoon yeast and 3 cups flour. Since this is a one-third decrease in the flour, also decrease the remaining ingredients by one-third.
- If a bread uses 2 or more types of flour, add the flour amounts together and use that total as the basis for reducing the recipe. The total amount of flour used should be only 3 or 4 cups, depending on the size of your loaf.
- Use bread flour instead of all-purpose flour or add 1 to 3 tablespoons gluten flour (available at health-food stores) to the all-purpose flour. If your recipe contains any rye flour, add 1 tablespoon of gluten flour even when bread flour is used.

- Add ingredients in the order specified by the bread machine manufacturer.
- Add dried fruits or nuts at the raisin bread cycle, if your machine has one. If it doesn't, add them according to the manufacturer's directions.
- Don't use light-colored dried fruits, such as apricots or golden raisins, because preservatives added to these dried fruits inhibit yeast performance. Choose another fruit or use only the dough cycle of your machine, lightly knead in the fruit by hand before shaping the bread, then bake it in the oven.
- When making dough to shape by hand, you may want to knead in a little more flour after removing the dough from the machine. Knead in just enough additional flour to make the dough easy to handle.
- For breads made with whole wheat or rye flour or other whole grains, use the whole grain cycle, if your machine has one.
- For sweet or rich breads, first try the light-crust color setting or sweet bread cycle, if available.
- Follow the directions for "Checking Dough Consistency" on page 10. For future reference, record how much additional liquid or flour you added.

NUTRITION FACTS

All of the recipes in this book include a nutrition analysis. The calculations are for 1 slice or serving of the 1½-pound recipe. You'll find the calorie count and the amount of fat, saturated fat, cholesterol, sodium, carbohydrates, fiber, and protein for each serving. Each of these, except protein, is noted also as a percentage of the Daily Values (dietary standards set by the U.S. Food and Drug Administration).

The dietary guidelines below suggest nutrient levels that moderately active adults should strive to eat each day. As your calorie levels change, adjust your fat intake, too. Try to keep the percentage of calories from fat to no more than 30 percent. There's no harm in occasionally going over or under these guidelines, but the key to good health is maintaining a balanced diet *most of the time.*

Calories: about 2,000
Total fat: <65 grams
Saturated fat: <20 grams
Cholesterol: <300 milligrams
Carbohydrates: about 300 grams
Sodium: <2,400 milligrams
Dietary fiber: 20 to 30 grams

The Better Homes and Gardens Test Kitchen computer analyzes each recipe for the nutritional value of a single serving.
- *The analysis does not include optional ingredients.*
- *We use the first serving size listed when a range is given. For example: If we say a recipe "Makes 4 to 6 servings," the Nutrition Facts are based on 4 servings.*
- *When ingredient choices (such as margarine or butter) appear in a recipe, we use the first one mentioned for analysis. The ingredient order does not mean we prefer one ingredient over another.*
- *When milk is a recipe ingredient, the analysis is calculated using 2-percent milk.*

$\mathcal{P}$LAIN AND SIMPLE

At left: *Egg Bread*

WHITE BREAD

The golden crust, tender texture, and delicate flavor of this basic bread earned hearty praise from our panel of tasters.

1½-pound (16 slices)	Ingredients	2-pound (22 slices)
1 cup	milk	1¼ cups
¼ cup	water*	¼ cup
4 teaspoons	margarine, butter, or olive oil	2 tablespoons
3 cups	bread flour	4 cups
4 teaspoons	sugar	2 tablespoons
¾ teaspoon	salt	1 teaspoon
1 teaspoon	active dry yeast or bread machine yeast	1¼ teaspoons

NUTRITION FACTS PER SLICE

		Daily Values
Calories	114	5%
Total fat	2 g	2%
Sat. fat	<0.5 g	2%
Cholesterol	1 mg	0%
Sodium	119 mg	4%
Carbo.	21 g	6%
Fiber	1 g	3%
Protein	4 g	

Select the loaf size. Add the ingredients to the machine according to the manufacturer's directions. Select the basic white bread cycle.

*Note: Our Test Kitchen recommends ¼ cup water for either size loaf.

WHOLE WHEAT BREAD

1½-pound (16 slices)	Ingredients	2-pound (22 slices)
1 cup	milk	1⅓ cups
3 tablespoons	water	¼ cup
4 teaspoons	honey or sugar	2 tablespoons
1 tablespoon	margarine or butter	4 teaspoons
1½ cups	whole wheat flour	2 cups
1½ cups	bread flour	2 cups
¾ teaspoon	salt	1 teaspoon
1 teaspoon	active dry yeast or bread machine yeast	1¼ teaspoons

Whole wheat flour and honey give this tender loaf a nutty, slightly sweet taste that's irresistible. Try it toasted and spread with raspberry jam.

Select the loaf size. Add the ingredients to the machine according to the manufacturer's directions. If available, select the whole grain cycle, or select the basic white bread cycle.

NUTRITION FACTS PER SLICE		Daily Values
Calories	105	5%
Total fat	1 g	2%
Sat. fat	<0.5 g	1%
Cholesterol	1 mg	0%
Sodium	117 mg	4%
Carbo.	20 g	6%
Fiber	2 g	7%
Protein	4 g	

EGG BREAD

Thanks to the featured ingredient, this crusty loaf has a rich, savory quality and a beautiful golden color.

Pictured on page 18.

1½-pound* (20 slices)	Ingredients	2-pound* (27 slices)
¾ cup	milk**	¾ cup
¼ cup	water	⅓ cup
1	egg(s)	2
2 tablespoons	margarine or butter**	2 tablespoons
3 cups	bread flour	4 cups
2 tablespoons	sugar	3 tablespoons
¾ teaspoon	salt	1 teaspoon
1 teaspoon	active dry yeast or bread machine yeast	1¼ teaspoons

NUTRITION FACTS PER SLICE		Daily Values
Calories	98	4%
Total fat	2 g	2%
Sat. fat	<0.5 g	2%
Cholesterol	11 mg	3%
Sodium	102 mg	4%
Carbo.	17 g	5%
Fiber	1 g	2%
Protein	3 g	

Select the loaf size. Add the ingredients to the machine according to the manufacturer's directions. Select the basic white bread cycle.

*Note: For the 1½-pound loaf, the bread machine pan must have a capacity of 10 cups or more. For the 2-pound loaf, the bread machine pan must have a capacity of 12 cups or more.

**Note: Our Test Kitchen recommends ¾ cup milk and 2 tablespoons margarine or butter for either size loaf.

POTATO BREAD

1½-pound* (16 slices)	Ingredients	2-pound* (22 slices)
½ cup	water	⅔ cup
⅔ cup	milk	¾ cup
1	egg**	1
2 tablespoons	margarine or butter, cut up, or shortening	3 tablespoons
3 cups	bread flour	4 cups
½ cup	packaged instant mashed potato flakes or buds	⅔ cup
1 tablespoon	sugar	4 teaspoons
¾ teaspoon	salt	1 teaspoon
1 teaspoon	active dry yeast or bread machine yeast	1¼ teaspoons

Ideal as an accompaniment for soups and stews, this home-style bread is made with instant mashed potatoes for moist, rich flavor.

Select the loaf size. Add the ingredients to the machine according to the manufacturer's directions. Select the basic white bread cycle.

*Note: For the 1½-pound loaf, the bread machine pan must have a capacity of 10 cups or more. For the 2-pound loaf, the bread machine pan must have a capacity of 12 cups or more.

**Note: Our Test Kitchen recommends 1 egg for either size loaf.

NUTRITION FACTS PER SLICE		Daily Values
Calories	124	6%
Total fat	2 g	3%
Sat. fat	1 g	2%
Cholesterol	14 mg	4%
Sodium	128 mg	5%
Carbo.	21 g	7%
Fiber	1 g	3%
Protein	4 g	

BUTTERMILK BREAD

Take a loaf of this pleasantly tangy bread to your next family get-together or potluck.

1½-pound (16 slices)	Ingredients	2-pound (22 slices)
1 cup	buttermilk	1⅓ cups
¼ cup	water	⅓ cup
2 teaspoons	margarine, butter, or cooking oil	1 tablespoon
3 cups	bread flour	4 cups
2 tablespoons	toasted wheat germ	3 tablespoons
1 tablespoon	sugar	4 teaspoons
¾ teaspoon	salt	1 teaspoon
1 teaspoon	active dry yeast or bread machine yeast	1¼ teaspoons

NUTRITION FACTS PER SLICE		Daily Values
Calories	110	5%
Total fat	1 g	1%
Sat. fat	<0.5 g	1%
Cholesterol	1 mg	0%
Sodium	122 mg	5%
Carbo.	21 g	6%
Fiber	1 g	3%
Protein	4 g	

Select the loaf size. Add the ingredients to the machine according to the manufacturer's directions. Select the basic white bread cycle.

CHEESE BREAD

1½-pound* (16 slices)	Ingredients	2-pound (22 slices)
⅔ cup	milk	¾ cup
¼ cup	water	½ cup
1	egg**	1
3 cups	bread flour	4 cups
1¼ cups (5 ounces)	shredded cheddar cheese or Monterey Jack cheese with jalapeño peppers	1⅔ cups (about 7 ounces)
2 tablespoons	sugar	3 tablespoons
¾ teaspoon	salt	1 teaspoon
1 teaspoon	active dry yeast or bread machine yeast	1¼ teaspoons

Cheese adds gusto to this exceptional loaf. For variety, make it with equal parts cheddar cheese and Monterey Jack cheese (with or without jalapeño peppers).

Select the loaf size. Add the ingredients to the machine according to the manufacturer's directions. Select the basic white bread cycle. If available, try the light-crust color setting.

*Note: For the 1½-pound loaf, the bread machine pan must have a capacity of 10 cups or more.

**Note: Our Test Kitchen recommends 1 egg for either size loaf.

NUTRITION FACTS PER SLICE		
		Daily Values
Calories	145	7%
Total fat	4 g	5%
Sat. fat	2 g	10%
Cholesterol	23 mg	7%
Sodium	164 mg	6%
Carbo.	21 g	6%
Fiber	1 g	3%
Protein	6 g	

BEER BREAD

To guarantee a light, even-textured loaf, allow the starter for this bold-flavored bread to stand in a warm place for 12 to 24 hours.

1½-pound* (24 slices)	Ingredients	2-pound* (32 slices)
¾ cup	beer	1 cup
4 teaspoons	brown sugar	2 tablespoons
1 teaspoon	active dry yeast**	1 teaspoon
1 cup	bread flour	1⅓ cups
⅓ cup	milk	½ cup
1	egg**	1
4 teaspoons	olive oil or cooking oil	2 tablespoons
2 cups	bread flour	2⅔ cups
¾ teaspoon	salt	1 teaspoon
1 teaspoon	active dry yeast or bread machine yeast	1¼ teaspoons

NUTRITION FACTS PER SLICE		
		Daily Values
Calories	80	3%
Total fat	1 g	2%
Sat. fat	<0.5 g	1%
Cholesterol	9 mg	3%
Sodium	72 mg	2%
Carbo.	14 g	4%
Fiber	1 g	2%
Protein	3 g	

For the starter: Select the loaf size. In a medium mixing bowl combine the beer and brown sugar. Sprinkle the 1 teaspoon yeast over beer mixture; stir to dissolve. Stir in the first bread flour, using 1 cup for the 1½-pound loaf and 1⅓ cups for the 2-pound loaf. Mix well. Cover with plastic wrap; let stand at room temperature (75° to 85°) for 12 to 24 hours.

To finish the bread: Add the starter and the remaining ingredients to the machine according to the manufacturer's directions. Select the basic white bread cycle.

*Note: For the 1½-pound loaf, the bread machine pan must have a capacity of 10 cups or more. For the 2-pound loaf, the bread machine pan must have a capacity of 12 cups or more.

**Note: For the starter, our Test Kitchen recommends 1 teaspoon yeast for either size loaf. Also, our Test Kitchen recommends 1 egg for either size loaf.

RYE BREAD

1½-pound (16 slices)	Ingredients	2-pound (22 slices)
1 cup	water	1⅓ cups
2 tablespoons	margarine or butter, cut up, or shortening or cooking oil	3 tablespoons
2 cups	bread flour	2⅔ cups
1 cup	rye flour	1⅓ cups
2 tablespoons	gluten flour	3 tablespoons
2 tablespoons	brown sugar	3 tablespoons
1½ teaspoons	caraway seed (optional)	2 teaspoons
¾ teaspoon	salt	1 teaspoon
1 teaspoon	active dry yeast or bread machine yeast	1¼ teaspoons

As we tested the recipes for this book, we found that gluten flour is essential for tender, even-textured rye breads. Without it, the loaves tend to be dense and compact. (See gluten flour in glossary, page 13.)

Select the loaf size. Add the ingredients to the machine according to the manufacturer's directions. If available, select the whole grain cycle, or select the basic white bread cycle.

NUTRITION FACTS PER SLICE		
		Daily Values
Calories	108	5%
Total fat	2 g	2%
Sat. fat	<0.5 g	1%
Cholesterol	0 mg	0%
Sodium	118 mg	4%
Carbo.	20 g	6%
Fiber	2 g	6%
Protein	3 g	

SOURDOUGHS

At left: *Pepper-Parmesan Sourdough Bread*

SOURDOUGH STARTER

You'll be ready to make sourdough bread whenever you like if you keep this simple starter on hand. Unlike the other recipes in this book, the starter should be made with all-purpose flour. Using bread flour will give the starter a stringy quality.

Amount	Ingredients
1½ teaspoons	active dry yeast or bread machine yeast
¾ cup	warm water (105° to 115°)
3 cups	warm water (105° to 115°)
3 cups	all-purpose flour
4 teaspoons	granulated sugar or brown sugar

To make the starter: Dissolve the yeast in ¾ cup warm water. Stir in 3 cups warm water, the flour, and sugar. Beat with an electric mixer on medium speed until smooth.

Cover with 100-percent-cotton cheesecloth. Let stand at room temperature (75° to 85°) for 5 to 10 days or until the mixture has a sour, fermented aroma, stirring 2 or 3 times every day. (The fermentation time will depend upon the room temperature. A warmer room speeds the fermentation process.) When the mixture has fermented, transfer starter to a 2-quart or larger covered plastic container. Refrigerate the starter until needed.

To use the starter: Stir the starter thoroughly upon removing it from the refrigerator, then measure the amount needed and bring it to room temperature before using. (The cold starter should be the consistency of buttermilk or thin pancake batter. If necessary, add water to thin the starter after you have stirred it and before it is measured.)

For each cup of starter used, replenish the remaining starter by adding ¾ cup all-purpose flour, ¾ cup water, and 1 teaspoon granulated or brown sugar. Cover and let mixture stand at room temperature for at least 1 day or until it is bubbly. Refrigerate starter for later use.

If you have not used the starter within 10 days, stir in 1 teaspoon granulated or brown sugar. Repeat every 10 days unless starter is replenished. Makes about 4 cups.

SAN FRANCISCO-STYLE SOURDOUGH BREAD

1½-pound (20 slices)	Ingredients	2-pound (27 slices)
1¼ cups	Sourdough Starter	1¾ cups
2 tablespoons	milk	¼ cup
3 cups	bread flour	4 cups
1 tablespoon	sugar	4 teaspoons
¾ teaspoon	salt	1 teaspoon
1 teaspoon	active dry yeast or bread machine yeast	1¼ teaspoons
	cornmeal	

During the days of the California gold rush, bakers in San Francisco staked their reputations on baking exceptional sourdough breads such as this one.

Select the loaf size. Add all of the ingredients except cornmeal to the machine according to the manufacturer's directions. Select the dough cycle. When the cycle is complete, remove the dough from the machine. Cover and let rest for 10 minutes.

Lightly grease baking sheet(s); sprinkle with cornmeal. Set aside. On a lightly floured surface, shape the 1½-pound dough into one 8-inch round loaf or divide the 2-pound dough in half and shape each half into a 6-inch round or an 8×4-inch oval loaf.

Place loaf (loaves) on prepared baking sheet(s). Using a sharp knife, slash top(s) of loaf (loaves) diagonally. Cover and let rise in a warm place for 30 to 45 minutes or until nearly double.

Brush top(s) with water. Bake in a 400° oven for 20 to 30 minutes or until crust of each is golden brown and bread sounds hollow when tapped. Remove from oven; cool on wire rack(s).

NUTRITION FACTS PER SLICE		Daily Values
Calories	102	5%
Total fat	0 g	0%
Sat. fat	0 g	0%
Cholesterol	0 mg	0%
Sodium	82 mg	3%
Carbo.	21 g	6%
Fiber	1 g	3%
Protein	3 g	

PEPPER-PARMESAN SOURDOUGH BREAD

The sharp flavors of black pepper and Parmesan cheese complement this loaf's tangy sourdough taste.

Pictured on page 28.

1½-pound* (20 slices)	Ingredients	2-pound* (27 slices)
1 cup	Sourdough Starter	1⅓ cups
½ cup	water	⅔ cup
1 tablespoon	margarine or butter	4 teaspoons
2½ cups	bread flour	3⅓ cups
½ cup	whole wheat flour	⅔ cup
⅓ cup	grated Parmesan cheese	½ cup
¾ teaspoon	salt	1 teaspoon
¾ teaspoon	cracked black pepper	1 teaspoon
1 teaspoon	active dry yeast or bread machine yeast**	1 teaspoon

Select the loaf size. Add the ingredients to the machine according to the manufacturer's directions. Select the basic white bread cycle.

*Note: For the 1½-pound loaf, the bread machine pan must have a capacity of 10 cups or more. For the 2-pound loaf, the bread machine pan must have a capacity of 12 cups or more.

**Note: Our Test Kitchen recommends 1 teaspoon yeast for either size loaf.

GARLIC SOURDOUGH BREAD

1½-pound (16 slices)	Ingredients	2-pound (22 slices)
2 tablespoons	thinly sliced green onion	3 tablespoons
2 cloves	garlic, minced	3 cloves
¾ teaspoon	dried Italian seasoning, crushed	1 teaspoon
2 tablespoons	olive oil or cooking oil*	2 tablespoons
1 cup	Sourdough Starter	1⅓ cups
⅓ cup	water	½ cup
3 cups	bread flour	4 cups
1 tablespoon	sugar	4 teaspoons
¾ teaspoon	salt	1 teaspoon
1 teaspoon	active dry yeast or bread machine yeast	1¼ teaspoons

Seasoned with garlic, Italian spices, and olive oil, this robust loaf is an ideal accompaniment for lasagna or spaghetti with meat sauce.

Select the loaf size. In a small skillet cook green onion, garlic, and Italian seasoning in hot oil for 2 to 3 minutes or until green onion is tender, stirring occasionally. Cool slightly. Add green onion mixture and the remaining ingredients to the machine according to the manufacturer's directions. Select the basic white bread cycle.

*Note: Our Test Kitchen recommends 2 tablespoons olive oil or cooking oil for either size loaf.

NUTRITION FACTS PER SLICE		Daily Values
Calories	135	6%
Total fat	2 g	3%
Sat. fat	<0.5 g	1%
Cholesterol	0 mg	0%
Sodium	101 mg	4%
Carbo.	24 g	8%
Fiber	1 g	4%
Protein	4 g	

RAISIN-ALMOND SOURDOUGH BREAD

Save leftover slices of this extraordinary raisin bread to make scrumptious French toast.

1½-pound* (20 slices)	Ingredients	2-pound* (27 slices)
1 cup	Sourdough Starter	1⅓ cups
⅓ cup	water	½ cup
2 tablespoons	honey	3 tablespoons
1	egg**	1
1 tablespoon	margarine, butter, or shortening	2 tablespoons
3 cups	bread flour	4 cups
1 teaspoon	finely shredded orange peel	1½ teaspoons
¾ teaspoon	salt	1 teaspoon
½ cup	chopped toasted blanched almonds	⅔ cup
½ cup	dark raisins	⅔ cup
1 teaspoon	active dry yeast or bread machine yeast**	1 teaspoon

NUTRITION FACTS PER SLICE		
		Daily Values
Calories	134	6%
Total fat	3 g	3%
Sat. fat	<0.5 g	1%
Cholesterol	11 mg	3%
Sodium	91 mg	3%
Carbo.	24 g	8%
Fiber	1 g	5%
Protein	4 g	

Select the loaf size. Add the ingredients to the machine according to the manufacturer's directions. Select the basic white bread cycle.

*Note: For the 1½-pound loaf, the bread machine pan must have a capacity of 10 cups or more. For the 2-pound loaf, the bread machine pan must have a capacity of 12 cups or more.

**Note: Our Test Kitchen recommends 1 egg and 1 teaspoon yeast for either size loaf.

MULTIGRAIN SOURDOUGH BREAD

1½-pound (16 slices)	Ingredients	2-pound (22 slices)
1¼ cups	Sourdough Starter	1½ cups
¼ cup	milk	½ cup
1 tablespoon	honey	2 tablespoons
1 tablespoon	margarine, butter, shortening, or cooking oil	2 tablespoons
1¼ cups	whole wheat flour	1⅔ cups
1 cup	bread flour	1⅓ cups
½ cup	rye flour	⅔ cup
¼ cup	cornmeal	⅓ cup
2 tablespoons	gluten flour*	2 tablespoons
1 teaspoon	fennel seed	1½ teaspoons
¾ teaspoon	salt	1 teaspoon
1 teaspoon	active dry yeast or bread machine yeast	1¼ teaspoons

This chewy sandwich bread boasts cornmeal and three kinds of flour, but it's the fennel seed's hint of licorice flavor that makes the bread unique.

Select the loaf size. Add the ingredients to the machine according to the manufacturer's directions. If available, select the whole grain cycle, or select the basic white bread cycle.

*Note: Our Test Kitchen recommends 2 tablespoons gluten flour for either size loaf.

NUTRITION FACTS PER SLICE		
		Daily Values
Calories	128	6%
Total fat	1 g	2%
Sat. fat	<0.5 g	1%
Cholesterol	0 mg	0%
Sodium	112 mg	4%
Carbo.	25 g	8%
Fiber	2 g	9%
Protein	4 g	

Whole Grain Goodness

At left: *Onion-Millet Bread*

WHOLE GRAIN BREAD

Four-grain cereal and sunflower seeds put this loaf a cut above ordinary whole wheat bread.

1½-pound (16 slices)	Ingredients	2-pound (22 slices)
¾ cup	milk	1 cup
⅓ cup	water	½ cup
1 tablespoon	honey or molasses	4 teaspoons
1 tablespoon	margarine, butter, or shortening	4 teaspoons
2 cups	bread flour	2⅔ cups
1 cup	whole wheat flour	1⅓ cups
¾ cup	four-grain cereal flakes	1 cup
⅓ cup	shelled unsalted sunflower seeds or chopped pecans	½ cup
½ teaspoon	salt	¾ teaspoon
1 teaspoon	active dry yeast or bread machine yeast	1¼ teaspoons

Select the loaf size. Add the ingredients to the machine according to the manufacturer's directions. If available, select the whole grain cycle, or select the basic white bread cycle.

NUTRITION FACTS PER SLICE		
		Daily Values
Calories	126	6%
Total fat	3 g	4%
Sat. fat	<0.5 g	2%
Cholesterol	1 mg	0%
Sodium	97 mg	4%
Carbo.	21 g	7%
Fiber	2 g	7%
Protein	4 g	

FOUR-GRAIN BREAD

1½-pound (16 slices)	Ingredients	2-pound (22 slices)
⅓ cup	quick-cooking rolled oats	½ cup
⅓ cup	quick-cooking barley	½ cup
1¼ cups	water	1⅔ cups
2 tablespoons	margarine or butter, cut up, or cooking oil	3 tablespoons
1½ cups	bread flour	1⅔ cups
¾ cup	whole wheat flour	1 cup
⅓ cup	cornmeal	½ cup
1 tablespoon	gluten flour	4 teaspoons
1 tablespoon	sugar	2 tablespoons
¾ teaspoon	salt	1 teaspoon
1¼ teaspoons	active dry yeast or bread machine yeast	1½ teaspoons

Wheat, oats, barley, and corn offer robust flavor in this nutritious loaf.

Select the loaf size. Spread the rolled oats and barley in a shallow baking pan. Bake in a 350° oven about 15 minutes or until light brown, stirring occasionally. Let cool. Place the toasted oats and barley in a blender container. Cover and blend until the mixture is the consistency of flour. Add the mixture and the remaining ingredients to the bread machine according to the manufacturer's directions. If available, select whole grain cycle, or select the basic white bread cycle.

NUTRITION FACTS PER SLICE		
		Daily Values
Calories	123	6%
Total fat	2 g	3%
Sat. fat	<0.5 g	1%
Cholesterol	0 mg	0%
Sodium	118 mg	4%
Carbo.	23 g	7%
Fiber	2 g	6%
Protein	4 g	

HARVEST BREAD

Toasted wheat germ gives this top-notch bread a slightly nutty flavor.

1½-pound (16 slices)	Ingredients	2-pound (22 slices)
1 cup	milk	1⅓ cups
1	egg(s)	2
2 tablespoons	margarine or butter, cut up	3 tablespoons
2½ cups	bread flour	3⅓ cups
¾ cup	whole wheat flour	1 cup
½ cup	toasted wheat germ	⅔ cup
3 tablespoons	packed brown sugar	¼ cup
¾ teaspoon	salt	1 teaspoon
1 teaspoon	active dry yeast or bread machine yeast	1¼ teaspoons

NUTRITION FACTS PER SLICE		Daily Values
Calories	143	7%
Total fat	3 g	4%
Sat. fat	1 g	3%
Cholesterol	14 mg	4%
Sodium	130 mg	5%
Carbo.	24 g	8%
Fiber	1 g	5%
Protein	5 g	

Select the loaf size. Add the ingredients to the machine according to the manufacturer's directions. If available, select the whole grain cycle, or select the basic white bread cycle.

HONEY-GRAIN BREAD

1½-pound (16 slices)	Ingredients	2-pound (22 slices)
1 cup	water	1⅓ cups
3 tablespoons	honey	¼ cup
2 tablespoons	margarine or butter, cut up	3 tablespoons
1⅔ cups	bread flour	2¼ cups
1⅓ cups	whole wheat flour	1⅔ cups
¾ cup	muesli	1 cup
¾ teaspoon	salt	1 teaspoon
¼ teaspoon	ground cinnamon	½ teaspoon
1 teaspoon	active dry yeast or bread machine yeast	1¼ teaspoons

Bursting with flavor and nutrition, this loaf includes muesli, a tempting combination of rolled oats mixed with other cereals or grains, dried fruits, and nuts. Look for muesli in the cereal aisle of your supermarket.

Pictured on the cover and page 4.

Select the loaf size. Add the ingredients to the machine according to the manufacturer's directions. If available, select the whole grain cycle, or select the basic white bread cycle. If available, try the light-crust color setting.

NUTRITION FACTS PER SLICE		Daily Values
Calories	133	6%
Total fat	2 g	3%
Sat. fat	<0.5 g	2%
Cholesterol	0 mg	0%
Sodium	130 mg	5%
Carbo.	25 g	8%
Fiber	2 g	9%
Protein	4 g	

OATMEAL BREAD

For a satisfying sandwich, team this stout bread with your favorite chicken or tuna salad and a crisp lettuce leaf.

1½-pound (16 slices)	Ingredients	2-pound (22 slices)
1 cup	quick-cooking rolled oats	1⅓ cups
⅔ cup	milk	¾ cup
⅓ cup	water	½ cup
1 tablespoon	margarine, butter, or shortening	2 tablespoons
2½ cups	bread flour	3⅓ cups
3 tablespoons	packed brown sugar	¼ cup
¾ teaspoon	salt	1 teaspoon
1 teaspoon	active dry yeast or bread machine yeast	1¼ teaspoons

NUTRITION FACTS PER SLICE		
		Daily Values
Calories	117	5%
Total fat	2 g	2%
Sat. fat	<0.5 g	1%
Cholesterol	1 mg	0%
Sodium	115 mg	4%
Carbo.	22 g	7%
Fiber	1 g	4%
Protein	4 g	

Select the loaf size. Spread the oats in a shallow baking pan. Bake in a 350° oven for 15 to 20 minutes or until light brown, stirring occasionally. Cool. Add the oats and the remaining ingredients to the machine according to the manufacturer's directions. If available, select whole grain cycle, or select the basic white bread cycle.

RYE-ANISE LOAF

1½-pound (16 slices)	Ingredients	2-pound (22 slices)
½ cup	milk	¾ cup
¼ cup	water	⅓ cup
1	egg*	1
2 tablespoons	margarine or butter, cut up, or shortening	3 tablespoons
2 cups	bread flour	2⅔ cups
1 cup	rye flour	1⅔ cups
3 tablespoons	packed brown sugar	¼ cup
1 tablespoon	gluten flour	4 teaspoons
2 teaspoons	aniseed, slightly crushed	1 tablespoon
1½ teaspoons	finely shredded orange peel	2 teaspoons
¾ teaspoon	salt	1 teaspoon
1½ teaspoons	active dry yeast or bread machine yeast	1¾ teaspoons

This first-rate loaf is ideal for deli-style corned beef or pastrami sandwiches.

Select the loaf size. Add the ingredients to the machine according to the manufacturer's directions. If available, select the whole grain cycle, or select the basic white bread cycle. If available, try the light-crust color setting.

*Note: Our Test Kitchen recommends 1 egg for either size loaf.

NUTRITION FACTS PER SLICE		
		Daily Values
Calories	118	5%
Total fat	2 g	3%
Sat. fat	1 g	2%
Cholesterol	14 mg	4%
Sodium	126 mg	5%
Carbo.	20 g	6%
Fiber	1 g	5%
Protein	4 g	

YOGURT CORN BREAD

Cornmeal and whole kernel corn color this loaf golden; yogurt lends a delightful sourdoughlike tang.

1½-pound (20 slices)	Ingredients	2-pound (27 slices)
¾ cup	plain low-fat yogurt	1 cup
⅓ cup	water	½ cup
1 tablespoon	margarine or butter	4 teaspoons
2½ cups	bread flour	3⅓ cups
¾ cup	cornmeal	1 cup
¾ cup	canned whole kernel corn, well drained	1 cup
2 teaspoons	sugar	1 tablespoon
1 teaspoon	onion powder	1½ teaspoons
¾ teaspoon	salt	1 teaspoon
1 teaspoon	active dry yeast or bread machine yeast	1¼ teaspoons

NUTRITION FACTS PER SLICE		Daily Values
Calories	99	4%
Total fat	1 g	1%
Sat. fat	<0.5 g	1%
Cholesterol	1 mg	0%
Sodium	113 mg	4%
Carbo.	19 g	6%
Fiber	1 g	3%
Protein	3 g	

Select the loaf size. Add the ingredients to the machine according to the manufacturer's directions. If available, select the whole grain cycle, or select the basic white bread cycle.

LEMONY GRANOLA BREAD

1½-pound* (16 slices)	Ingredients	2-pound (22 slices)
1¼ cups	water	1½ cups
3 tablespoons	margarine or butter, cut up	¼ cup
2 cups	bread flour	2⅔ cups
1 cup	whole wheat flour	1⅓ cups
1½ cups	granola with raisins	2 cups
¼ cup	nonfat dry milk powder	⅓ cup
1 teaspoon	finely shredded lemon peel	1½ teaspoons
¾ teaspoon	salt	1 teaspoon
1 teaspoon	active dry yeast or bread machine yeast	1¼ teaspoons

As you shred the lemon peel for this fresh-tasting bread, use only the yellow outer peel; the white part is too bitter.

Select the loaf size. Add the ingredients to the machine according to the manufacturer's directions. If available, select the whole grain cycle, or select the basic white bread cycle.

*Note: For the 1½-pound loaf, the bread machine pan must have a capacity of 10 cups or more.

NUTRITION FACTS PER SLICE		
		Daily Values
Calories	158	7%
Total fat	4 g	6%
Sat. fat	2 g	8%
Cholesterol	0 mg	0%
Sodium	154 mg	6%
Carbo.	26 g	8%
Fiber	2 g	7%
Protein	5 g	

WILD RICE BREAD

The chewy texture and nutty, savory flavor of this bread come from the wild rice. It's great for turkey and cheese sandwiches.

1½-pound (16 slices)	Ingredients	2-pound (22 slices)
1 cup	water	1¼ cups
4 teaspoons	margarine or butter	2 tablespoons
2 cups	bread flour	2⅔ cups
1 cup	whole wheat flour	1⅓ cups
¾ cup	cooked wild rice, well drained and cooled*	1 cup
1 tablespoon	sugar	2 tablespoons
1¼ teaspoons	instant chicken bouillon granules	1½ teaspoons
¾ teaspoon	salt	1 teaspoon
½ teaspoon	dried thyme, crushed	1 teaspoon
1 teaspoon	active dry yeast or bread machine yeast	1¼ teaspoons

NUTRITION FACTS PER SLICE		
		Daily Values
Calories	108	5%
Total fat	1 g	2%
Sat. fat	<0.5 g	1%
Cholesterol	0 mg	0%
Sodium	180 mg	7%
Carbo.	20 g	6%
Fiber	2 g	6%
Protein	4 g	

Select the loaf size. Add the ingredients to the machine according to the manufacturer's directions. If available, select the whole grain cycle, or select the basic white bread cycle.

*Note: To get ¾ cup cooked wild rice, start with ¾ cup water and ¼ cup uncooked wild rice. To get 1 cup cooked wild rice, start with 1 cup water and ⅓ cup uncooked wild rice. In a small saucepan bring water to boiling; add wild rice. Reduce heat to low; simmer, covered, about 40 minutes or until rice is just tender. Drain well and cool completely.

ONION-MILLET BREAD

1½-pound (16 slices)	Ingredients	2-pound (22 slices)
1 cup	milk	1⅓ cups
2 tablespoons	water	3 tablespoons
1 tablespoon	cooking oil	4 teaspoons
2 cups	bread flour	2⅔ cups
1 cup	whole wheat flour	1⅓ cups
¼ cup	millet	⅓ cup
2 tablespoons	brown sugar	3 tablespoons
1 tablespoon	minced dried onion	4 teaspoons
¾ teaspoon	salt	1 teaspoon
⅛ teaspoon	garlic powder*	⅛ teaspoon
1 teaspoon	active dry yeast or bread machine yeast	1¼ teaspoons

Millet is a tiny round yellow cereal grain. It adds a chewy texture to this bread and a bit of nuttiness to the flavor. If you can't find it on your grocer's shelf, try a health-food store or Asian market. Millet will keep for up to 2 years stored in an airtight container in a cool, dry place.

Pictured on page 36.

Select the loaf size. Add the ingredients to the machine according to the manufacturer's directions. If available, select the whole grain cycle, or select the basic white bread cycle.

*Note: Our Test Kitchen recommends ⅛ teaspoon garlic powder for either size loaf.

NUTRITION FACTS PER SLICE

		Daily Values
Calories	121	6%
Total fat	2 g	2%
Sat. fat	<0.5 g	1%
Cholesterol	1 mg	0%
Sodium	109 mg	4%
Carbo.	23 g	7%
Fiber	2 g	7%
Protein	4 g	

Savory Loaves

At left: *Herbed Green Onion Bread*

WELSH RAREBIT BREAD

This distinctive bread captures the flavors of the classic British dish—a rich, well-seasoned cheese sauce made with beer or milk and served over toast.

1½-pound (16 slices)	Ingredients	2-pound (22 slices)
1 cup	milk	1⅓ cups
2 teaspoons	Worcestershire sauce	1 tablespoon
1 cup	shredded sharp cheddar cheese	1⅓ cups
2 teaspoons	margarine, butter, or cooking oil	1 tablespoon
3 cups	bread flour	4 cups
1 teaspoon	sugar	2 teaspoons
¾ teaspoon	salt	1 teaspoon
¾ teaspoon	dry mustard	1 teaspoon
⅛ teaspoon	ground red pepper	¼ teaspoon
1 teaspoon	active dry yeast or bread machine yeast	1¼ teaspoons

NUTRITION FACTS PER SLICE

		Daily Values
Calories	136	6%
Total fat	4 g	5%
Sat. fat	2 g	9%
Cholesterol	9 mg	2%
Sodium	164 mg	6%
Carbo.	20 g	6%
Fiber	1 g	3%
Protein	5 g	

Select the loaf size. Add the ingredients to the machine according to the manufacturer's directions. Select the basic white bread cycle.

HERBED GREEN ONION BREAD

1½-pound* (16 slices)	Ingredients	2-pound* (22 slices)
½ cup	thinly sliced green onions	¾ cup
½ teaspoon	dried basil, crushed	¾ teaspoon
½ teaspoon	dried thyme, crushed	¾ teaspoon
¼ teaspoon	dried rosemary, crushed**	¼ teaspoon
2 tablespoons	margarine or butter, cut up	3 tablespoons
1 cup	milk	1⅓ cups
1	egg**	1
3 cups	bread flour	4 cups
2 tablespoons	sugar	3 tablespoons
¾ teaspoon	salt	1 teaspoon
1 teaspoon	active dry yeast or bread machine yeast	1¼ teaspoons

If you grow your own herbs, take advantage of their fresh flavor by substituting them for the dried form in this onion loaf. For the 1½-pound loaf, use 1½ teaspoons each of snipped fresh basil and thyme, and ¾ teaspoon snipped rosemary. For the 2-pound loaf, use 2¼ teaspoons each snipped fresh basil and thyme, and ¾ teaspoon snipped rosemary.

Pictured on page 48.

Select the loaf size. In a small skillet cook green onions, basil, thyme, and rosemary in margarine or butter until green onions are tender, stirring occasionally. Cool slightly. Add green onion mixture and the remaining ingredients to the machine according to the manufacturer's directions. Select the basic white bread cycle.

To make breadsticks (as shown in the photograph on page 48), cut a thick slice of bread into 1-inch strips. Brush the bread with melted margarine or butter and additional herbs. Broil the breadsticks until golden brown, turning often.

*Note: For the 1½-pound loaf, the bread machine pan must have a capacity of 10 cups or more. For the 2-pound loaf, the bread machine pan must have a capacity of 12 cups or more.

**Note: Our Test Kitchen recommends ¼ teaspoon dried rosemary and 1 egg for either size loaf.

NUTRITION FACTS PER SLICE		Daily Values
Calories	125	6%
Total fat	2 g	3%
Sat. fat	1 g	3%
Cholesterol	14 mg	4%
Sodium	129 mg	5%
Carbo.	21 g	7%
Fiber	1 g	3%
Protein	4 g	

Bacon and Tomato Bread

For a perfect BLT, start with this bread that has bacon and tomato already baked into it.

1½-pound* (20 slices)	Ingredients	2-pound (27 slices)
1 cup	water	1⅓ cups
¼ cup	snipped dried tomatoes (oil-packed)	⅓ cup
1 tablespoon	olive oil or cooking oil	4 teaspoons
3 cups	bread flour	4 cups
¼ cup	cooked bacon pieces	⅓ cup
1 tablespoon	sugar	4 teaspoons
¾ teaspoon	salt	1 teaspoon
¾ teaspoon	dried basil, crushed	1 teaspoon
1 teaspoon	active dry yeast or bread machine yeast**	1 teaspoon

NUTRITION FACTS PER SLICE		Daily Values
Calories	92	4%
Total fat	2 g	2%
Sat. fat	<0.5 g	1%
Cholesterol	1 mg	0%
Sodium	99 mg	4%
Carbo.	16 g	5%
Fiber	1 g	2%
Protein	3 g	

Select the loaf size. Add the ingredients to the machine according to the manufacturer's directions. Select the basic white bread cycle.

*Note: For the 1½-pound loaf, the bread machine pan must have a capacity of 10 cups or more.

**Note: Our Test Kitchen recommends 1 teaspoon yeast for either size loaf.

GARDEN-PATCH BREAD

1½-pound (20 slices)	Ingredients	2-pound (27 slices)
½ cup	water	⅔ cup
⅓ cup	tomato juice	½ cup
½ cup	coarsely shredded carrots	⅔ cup
2 tablespoons	coarsely chopped green pepper	3 tablespoons
2 tablespoons	sliced green onion	3 tablespoons
1 tablespoon	margarine, butter, or cooking oil	4 teaspoons
3 cups	bread flour	4 cups
1 teaspoon	sugar	1½ teaspoons
¾ teaspoon	salt	1 teaspoon
¼ teaspoon	dried basil, crushed	½ teaspoon
1 teaspoon	active dry yeast or bread machine yeast*	1 teaspoon

This cream-of-the-crop loaf is perfect for toasted cheese sandwiches.

Select the loaf size. Add the ingredients to the machine according to the manufacturer's directions. Select the basic white bread cycle.

*Note: Our Test Kitchen recommends 1 teaspoon yeast for either size loaf.

NUTRITION FACTS PER SLICE		Daily Values
Calories	83	4%
Total fat	1 g	1%
Sat. fat	0 g	0%
Cholesterol	0 mg	0%
Sodium	102 mg	4%
Carbo.	16 g	5%
Fiber	1 g	3%
Protein	3 g	

GARLIC AND DRIED TOMATO BREAD

Bottled minced garlic is a handy substitute for fresh garlic cloves. Look for it in the produce section of your supermarket. Use 1½ teaspoons for the 1½-pound loaf and 2 teaspoons for the 2-pound loaf.

1½-pound* (16 slices)	Ingredients	2-pound* (22 slices)
1 cup	water	1⅓ cups
¼ cup	snipped dried tomatoes (not oil-packed)	⅓ cup
3 tablespoons	finely chopped onion	¼ cup
3	large cloves garlic	4
2 teaspoons	olive oil or cooking oil	1 tablespoon
2⅓ cups	bread flour	3 cups
⅔ cup	whole wheat flour	1 cup
2 teaspoons	sugar	1 tablespoon
¾ teaspoon	dried rosemary, crushed	1 teaspoon
¾ teaspoon	salt	1 teaspoon
1 teaspoon	active dry yeast or bread machine yeast	1¼ teaspoons

NUTRITION FACTS PER SLICE		
		Daily Values
Calories	101	5%
Total fat	1 g	1%
Sat. fat	0 g	0%
Cholesterol	0 mg	0%
Sodium	119 mg	4%
Carbo.	20 g	6%
Fiber	1 g	5%
Protein	3 g	

Select the loaf size. Add the ingredients to the machine according to the manufacturer's directions. Select the basic white bread cycle.

*Note: For the 1½-pound loaf, the bread machine pan must have a capacity of 10 cups or more. For the 2-pound loaf, the bread machine pan must have a capacity of 12 cups or more.

PROSCIUTTO LOAF

1½-pound* (16 slices)	Ingredients	2-pound* (22 slices)
½ cup	chopped onion	⅔ cup
1 tablespoon	olive oil or cooking oil	4 teaspoons
¾ cup	water	1 cup
1	egg(s)	2
3 cups	bread flour	4¼ cups
1 cup (5 ounces)	finely chopped prosciutto or Canadian-style bacon	1⅓ cups (7 ounces)
2 teaspoons	fennel seed, crushed	2½ teaspoons
½ teaspoon	salt	¾ teaspoon
¼ teaspoon	coarsely ground black pepper	½ teaspoon
1 teaspoon	active dry yeast or bread machine yeast	1¼ teaspoons

Distinctively Italian, prosciutto is ham that is seasoned and salt-cured, rather than smoked. It is typically sold cut into paper-thin slices. Look for it at your supermarket's deli counter.

Select the loaf size. In a small skillet cook the onion in hot oil until tender, stirring occasionally. Cool slightly (about 5 minutes). Add the onion mixture and the remaining ingredients to the machine according to the manufacturer's directions. Select the basic white bread cycle. Wrap any leftovers in plastic wrap and refrigerate.

*Note: For the 1½-pound loaf, the bread machine pan must have a capacity of 10 cups or more. For the 2-pound loaf, the bread machine pan must have a capacity of 12 cups or more.

NUTRITION FACTS PER SLICE		
		Daily Values
Calories	136	6%
Total fat	4 g	5%
Sat. fat	<0.5 g	1%
Cholesterol	13 mg	4%
Sodium	228 mg	9%
Carbo.	19 g	6%
Fiber	1 g	3%
Protein	6 g	

CARAWAY-CHEESE LOAF

To make extra-cheesy Reuben sandwiches, use this Swiss-cheese-laced bread instead of rye or pumpernickel. If you carry your lunch, save a slice to pack with tomato soup.

1½-pound* (16 slices)	Ingredients	2-pound* (22 slices)
¾ cup (3 ounces)	shredded Swiss cheese	1 cup (4 ounces)
3 tablespoons	bread flour	⅓ cup
1¼ cups	dark beer	1⅔ cups
1	egg**	1
3 cups	bread flour	4 cups
1 tablespoon	sugar	4 teaspoons
1 teaspoon	caraway seed, crushed	1¼ teaspoons
¾ teaspoon	salt	1 teaspoon
1 teaspoon	active dry yeast or bread machine yeast	1¼ teaspoons

NUTRITION FACTS PER SLICE		Daily Values
Calories	135	6%
Total fat	2 g	3%
Sat. fat	1 g	5%
Cholesterol	18 mg	6%
Sodium	119 mg	4%
Carbo.	22 g	7%
Fiber	1 g	3%
Protein	5 g	

Select the loaf size. In a small mixing bowl, toss together the Swiss cheese and the first bread flour (3 tablespoons for the 1½-pound recipe and ⅓ cup for the 2-pound recipe). Add the Swiss cheese mixture and the remaining ingredients to the machine according to the manufacturer's directions. Select the basic white bread cycle.

*Note: For the 1½-pound loaf, the bread machine pan must have a capacity of 10 cups or more. For the 2-pound loaf, the bread machine pan must have a capacity of 12 cups or more.

**Note: Our Test Kitchen recommends 1 egg for either size loaf.

BLUE CHEESE-POTATO BREAD

1½-pound* (20 slices)	Ingredients	2-pound (27 slices)
1¼ cups	water	1½ cups
1	egg**	1
1 tablespoon	margarine or butter	4 teaspoons
3 cups	bread flour	4 cups
⅓ cup	packaged instant mashed potato flakes or buds	½ cup
½ cup (2 ounces)	crumbled blue cheese	⅔ cup (about 2½ ounces)
¼ cup	nonfat dry milk powder	⅓ cup
1 tablespoon	sugar	4 teaspoons
¾ teaspoon	salt	1 teaspoon
½ teaspoon	onion powder	¾ teaspoon
1 teaspoon	active dry yeast or bread machine yeast**	1 teaspoon

This moist bread is a blue cheese lover's delight. Serve it with a chef's salad or creamy potato soup. For convenience, the recipe calls for instant potatoes.

Select the loaf size. Add the ingredients to the machine according to the manufacturer's directions. Select the basic white bread cycle.

*Note: For the 1½-pound loaf, the bread machine pan must have a capacity of 10 cups or more.

**Note: Our Test Kitchen recommends 1 egg and 1 teaspoon yeast for either size loaf.

NUTRITION FACTS PER SLICE		Daily Values
Calories	102	5%
Total fat	2 g	3%
Sat. fat	1 g	3%
Cholesterol	13 mg	4%
Sodium	136 mg	5%
Carbo.	17 g	5%
Fiber	1 g	2%
Protein	4 g	

PARMESAN-BACON LOAF

This bread spices up roast beef, pork, or turkey sandwiches. For maximum flavor, use fresh grated Parmesan cheese.

1½-pound* (20 slices)	Ingredients	2-pound (27 slices)
1 cup	milk	1⅓ cups
Several dashes	bottled hot pepper sauce	¼ teaspoon
1	egg**	1
3 cups	bread flour	4 cups
⅓ cup	grated Parmesan cheese	½ cup
2 tablespoons	cooked bacon pieces	3 tablespoons
½ teaspoon	salt	¾ teaspoon
1 teaspoon	active dry yeast or bread machine yeast	1¼ teaspoons

NUTRITION FACTS PER SLICE		Daily Values
Calories	94	4%
Total fat	1 g	2%
Sat. fat	1 g	2%
Cholesterol	13 mg	4%
Sodium	112 mg	4%
Carbo.	16 g	5%
Fiber	1 g	2%
Protein	4 g	

Select the loaf size. Add the ingredients to the machine according to the manufacturer's directions. Select the basic white bread cycle.

*Note: For the 1½-pound loaf, the bread machine pan must have a capacity of 10 cups or more.

**Note: Our Test Kitchen recommends 1 egg for either size loaf.

OLIVE BREAD

1½-pound	Ingredients	2-pound
(16 slices)		(22 slices)
1 cup	water	1¼ cups
¼ cup	chopped pimiento-stuffed green olives	⅓ cup
3 tablespoons	chopped ripe olives	¼ cup
2 teaspoons	olive oil or cooking oil	1 tablespoon
3 cups	bread flour	4 cups
2 teaspoons	sugar	1 tablespoon
1 teaspoon	dried Italian seasoning, crushed	1½ teaspoons
¾ teaspoon	salt	1 teaspoon
1 teaspoon	active dry yeast or bread machine yeast	1¼ teaspoons

Green olives, ripe olives, and olive oil make this fabulous bread a triple treat. Serve it with broiled pork chops or roast turkey breast and rice.

Select the loaf size. Add the ingredients to the machine according to the manufacturer's directions. Select the basic white bread cycle.

NUTRITION FACTS PER SLICE

		Daily Values
Calories	105	5%
Total fat	2 g	2%
Sat. fat	0 g	0%
Cholesterol	0 mg	0%
Sodium	148 mg	6%
Carbo.	19 g	6%
Fiber	1 g	3%
Protein	3 g	

A SWEET TOUCH

At left: *Café Almond Bread*

CAFÉ ALMOND BREAD

Flavored coffee powder lends this fanciful bread mocha and almond accents, plus creaminess and a hint of sweetness.

Pictured on page 62.

1½-pound* (20 slices)	Ingredients	2-pound (27 slices)
⅔ cup	milk	¾ cup
¼ cup	water	⅓ cup
1	egg**	1
2 tablespoons	margarine or butter, cut up	3 tablespoons
3 cups	bread flour	4 cups
3 tablespoons	sugar	¼ cup
2 tablespoons	instant Roman-style coffee powder	3 tablespoons
¾ teaspoon	salt	1 teaspoon
1 teaspoon	active dry yeast or bread machine yeast	1¼ teaspoons
½ cup	coarsely chopped blanched almonds, toasted	⅔ cup

NUTRITION FACTS PER SLICE		Daily Values
Calories	116	5%
Total fat	3 g	4%
Sat. fat	1 g	2%
Cholesterol	11 mg	3%
Sodium	101 mg	4%
Carbo.	18 g	6%
Fiber	1 g	3%
Protein	4 g	

Select the loaf size. Add the ingredients to the machine according to the manufacturer's directions. Select the basic white bread cycle. If available, try a light-crust color setting.

To make the tea breads in the photograph on page 62, use a small cookie cutter or canapé cutter to cut shapes from a slice of bread. Spread bread shapes with softened cream cheese and top with your choice of preserves, nuts, or fresh fruit such as raspberries, champagne grapes, or sliced strawberries.

*Note: For the 1½-pound loaf, the bread machine pan must have a capacity of 10 cups or more.

**Note: Our Test Kitchen recommends 1 egg for either size loaf.

CHOCOLATE-PEANUT LOAF

1½-pound* (16 slices)	Ingredients	2-pound* (22 slices)
¾ cup	milk	1 cup
3 tablespoons	water	¼ cup
3 tablespoons	honey	¼ cup
1 teaspoon	vanilla	1½ teaspoons
1	egg**	1
4 teaspoons	margarine or butter	2 tablespoons
3 cups	bread flour	4 cups
2 tablespoons	unsweetened cocoa powder	3 tablespoons
¾ teaspoon	salt	1 teaspoon
1 teaspoon	active dry yeast or bread machine yeast	1¼ teaspoons
½ cup	coarsely chopped peanuts	⅔ cup

Moist, tender, and full of nuts, this luscious loaf is destined for stardom with chocoholics. Serve it in place of doughnuts for a midmorning coffee break or with mugs of milk for an afternoon snack.

Select the loaf size. Add the ingredients to the machine according to the manufacturer's directions. Select the basic white bread cycle.

*Note: For the 1½-pound loaf, the bread machine pan must have a capacity of 10 cups or more. For the 2-pound loaf, the bread machine pan must have a capacity of 12 cups or more.

**Note: Our Test Kitchen recommends 1 egg for either size loaf.

NUTRITION FACTS PER SLICE		
		Daily Values
Calories	155	7%
Total fat	4 g	6%
Sat. fat	1 g	3%
Cholesterol	14 mg	4%
Sodium	159 mg	6%
Carbo.	24 g	7%
Fiber	1 g	4%
Protein	5 g	

CHOCOLATE CHIP-COCONUT BREAD

Depending on how completely your bread machine melts the chocolate, this scrumptious loaf may be marbled, flecked, or uniform in color.

1½-pound* (16 slices)	Ingredients	2-pound* (22 slices)
¾ cup	milk	1 cup
2 tablespoons	water	3 tablespoons
1	egg**	1
1 teaspoon	vanilla	1½ teaspoons
1 tablespoon	margarine or butter	4 teaspoons
3 cups	bread flour	4 cups
2 tablespoons	sugar	3 tablespoons
¾ teaspoon	salt	1 teaspoon
1 teaspoon	active dry yeast or bread machine yeast	1¼ teaspoons
⅓ cup	semisweet chocolate pieces	½ cup
⅓ cup	toasted coconut	½ cup

NUTRITION FACTS PER SLICE		Daily Values
Calories	144	7%
Total fat	4 g	5%
Sat. fat	<0.5 g	2%
Cholesterol	14 mg	4%
Sodium	123 mg	5%
Carbo.	24 g	8%
Fiber	1 g	3%
Protein	4 g	

Select the loaf size. Add the ingredients to the machine according to the manufacturer's directions. Select the basic white bread cycle.

*Note: For the 1½-pound loaf, the bread machine pan must have a capacity of 10 cups or more. For the 2-pound loaf, the bread machine pan must have a capacity of 12 cups or more.

**Note: Our Test Kitchen recommends 1 egg for either size loaf.

HOLIDAY EGGNOG BREAD

1½-pound* (20 slices)	Ingredients	2-pound* (27 slices)
½ cup	canned or dairy eggnog	¾ cup
¼ cup	water	⅓ cup
1	egg**	1
2 tablespoons	margarine or butter, cut up	3 tablespoons
3 cups	bread flour	4 cups
2 tablespoons	sugar	3 tablespoons
¾ teaspoon	salt	1 teaspoon
¼ teaspoon	ground nutmeg	½ teaspoon
1¼ teaspoons	active dry yeast or bread machine yeast	1½ teaspoons
⅓ cup	mixed candied fruits and peels	½ cup
	Eggnog Glaze	

During the holidays, you'll find fresh eggnog in the dairy case of your supermarket. You can freeze it for up to 6 months to use later in the year or look for the canned version in the baking aisle or near the instant milk powder.

Select the loaf size. Add all of the ingredients except the Eggnog Glaze to the machine according to the manufacturer's directions. Select the basic white bread cycle. Drizzle cooled loaf with Eggnog Glaze.

Eggnog Glaze: In a small mixing bowl stir together 1 cup sifted *powdered sugar* and enough *canned* or *dairy eggnog* (1 to 2 tablespoons) to make a glaze of drizzling consistency.

*Note: For the 1½-pound loaf, the bread machine pan must have a capacity of 10 cups or more. For the 2-pound loaf, the bread machine pan must have a capacity of 12 cups or more.

**Note: Our Test Kitchen recommends 1 egg for either size loaf.

NUTRITION FACTS PER SLICE		
		Daily Values
Calories	133	6%
Total fat	2 g	3%
Sat. fat	<0.5 g	1%
Cholesterol	11 mg	3%
Sodium	102 mg	4%
Carbo.	25 g	8%
Fiber	1 g	2%
Protein	3 g	

HONEYED WALNUT BREAD

This delectable bread gets a double dose of walnut flavor from the walnut oil and toasted nuts. For an extra-special dessert, use some in your favorite bread pudding recipe.

1½-pound (20 slices)	Ingredients	2-pound (27 slices)
1 cup	water	1⅓ cups
¼ cup	honey	5 tablespoons
2 tablespoons	walnut oil or cooking oil	3 tablespoons
3 cups	bread flour	4 cups
¼ cup	nonfat dry milk powder	⅓ cup
¾ teaspoon	salt	1 teaspoon
1 teaspoon	active dry yeast or bread machine yeast	1¼ teaspoons
¾ cup	toasted coarsely chopped walnuts	1 cup

NUTRITION FACTS PER SLICE

		Daily Values
Calories	132	6%
Total fat	5 g	6%
Sat. fat	<0.5 g	2%
Cholesterol	0 mg	0%
Sodium	86 mg	3%
Carbo.	20 g	6%
Fiber	1 g	3%
Protein	3 g	

Select the loaf size. Add the ingredients to the machine according to the manufacturer's directions. Select the basic white bread cycle.

RAISIN-RUM LOAF

1½-pound* (16 slices)	Ingredients	2-pound* (22 slices)
½ cup	dark raisins	⅔ cup
3 tablespoons	dark or light rum	¼ cup
½ cup	dairy sour cream	⅔ cup
⅓ cup	water	½ cup
1 teaspoon	vanilla	1½ teaspoons
1	egg**	1
2 teaspoons	margarine or butter	1 tablespoon
3 cups	bread flour	4 cups
3 tablespoons	sugar	¼ cup
¾ teaspoon	salt	1 teaspoon
1 teaspoon	active dry yeast or bread machine yeast	1¼ teaspoons

The subtle flavor of rum complements the sweetness of raisins in this elegant bread. Toast thin slices for a special breakfast.

Select the loaf size. Add the ingredients to the machine according to the manufacturer's directions. Select the basic white bread cycle.

*Note: For the 1½-pound loaf, the bread machine pan must have a capacity of 10 cups or more. For the 2-pound loaf, the bread machine pan must have a capacity of 12 cups or more.

**Note: Our Test Kitchen recommends 1 egg for either size loaf.

NUTRITION FACTS PER SLICE		
		Daily Values
Calories	147	7%
Total fat	3 g	4%
Sat. fat	1 g	5%
Cholesterol	17 mg	5%
Sodium	114 mg	4%
Carbo.	25 g	8%
Fiber	1 g	4%
Protein	4 g	

ORANGE-CINNAMON LOAF

Showcase this golden loaf for brunch accompanied by your favorite orange marmalade.

1½-pound* (16 slices)	Ingredients	2-pound* (22 slices)
½ cup	buttermilk	⅔ cup
⅓ cup	water	½ cup
1	egg**	1
3 tablespoons	margarine or butter, cut up	¼ cup
3 cups	bread flour	4 cups
3 tablespoons	sugar	¼ cup
2 teaspoons	finely shredded orange peel	2½ teaspoons
¾ teaspoon	salt	1 teaspoon
¾ teaspoon	ground cinnamon	1 teaspoon
1 teaspoon	active dry yeast or bread machine yeast	1½ teaspoons
	Orange Glaze	

Select the loaf size. Add all of the ingredients except the Orange Glaze to the machine according to the manufacturer's directions. Select the basic white bread cycle. Drizzle cooled loaf with Orange Glaze.

Orange Glaze: In a small mixing bowl stir together 1 cup sifted *powdered sugar* and 1 teaspoon *vanilla*. Stir in enough *orange juice* (4 to 6 teaspoons) to make glaze of drizzling consistency.

*Note: For the 1½-pound loaf, the bread machine pan must have a capacity of 10 cups or more. For the 2-pound loaf, the bread machine pan must have a capacity of 12 cups or more.

**Note: Our Test Kitchen recommends 1 egg for either size loaf.

GINGERED LEMON BREAD

1½-pound* (20 slices)	Ingredients	2-pound* (27 slices)
¾ cup	milk	1 cup
2 tablespoons	water	¼ cup
1	egg**	1
2 tablespoons	margarine or butter, cut up	3 tablespoons
3 cups	bread flour	4 cups
2 tablespoons	brown sugar	3 tablespoons
¾ teaspoon	salt	1 teaspoon
1 teaspoon	active dry yeast or bread machine yeast	1¼ teaspoons
⅓ cup	coarsely chopped candied lemon peel	½ cup
2 tablespoons	coarsely chopped crystallized ginger	3 tablespoons

Candied lemon peel and crystallized ginger add a hint of sophistication to this delicate bread.

Select the loaf size. Add the ingredients to the machine according to the manufacturer's directions. Select the basic white bread cycle.

*Note: For the 1½-pound loaf, the bread machine pan must have a capacity of 10 cups or more. For the 2-pound loaf, the bread machine pan must have a capacity of 12 cups or more.

**Note: Our Test Kitchen recommends 1 egg for either size loaf.

NUTRITION FACTS PER SLICE		Daily Values
Calories	110	5%
Total fat	2 g	2%
Sat. fat	<0.5 g	2%
Cholesterol	11 mg	3%
Sodium	102 mg	4%
Carbo.	20 g	6%
Fiber	1 g	2%
Protein	3 g	

PUMPKIN-PECAN BREAD

This terrific nut bread combines the wonderful fall flavors of pumpkin pie and pecans.

1½-pound* (16 slices)	Ingredients	2-pound* (22 slices)
½ cup	milk	⅔ cup
½ cup	canned pumpkin	⅔ cup
1	egg**	1
2 tablespoons	margarine or butter, cut up	3 tablespoons
3 cups	bread flour	4 cups
3 tablespoons	packed brown sugar	¼ cup
¾ teaspoon	salt	1 teaspoon
¼ teaspoon	ground nutmeg	½ teaspoon
¼ teaspoon	ground ginger**	¼ teaspoon
⅛ teaspoon	ground cloves	¼ teaspoon
1 teaspoon	active dry yeast or bread machine yeast	1¼ teaspoons
¾ cup	coarsely chopped pecans	1 cup

NUTRITION FACTS PER SLICE		
		Daily Values
Calories	159	7%
Total fat	6 g	8%
Sat. fat	1 g	4%
Cholesterol	14 mg	4%
Sodium	126 mg	5%
Carbo.	23 g	7%
Fiber	1 g	5%
Protein	4 g	

Select the loaf size. Add the ingredients to the machine according to the manufacturer's directions. Select the basic white bread cycle.

*Note: For the 1½-pound loaf, the bread machine pan must have a capacity of 10 cups or more. For the 2-pound loaf, the bread machine pan must have a capacity of 12 cups or more.

**Note: Our Test Kitchen recommends 1 egg and ¼ teaspoon ground ginger for either size loaf.

PEACHES AND CREAM LOAF

1½-pound (16 slices)	Ingredients	2-pound (22 slices)
1 cup	strained peach baby food	1⅓ cups
3 tablespoons	whipping cream	¼ cup
¼ teaspoon	almond extract*	¼ teaspoon
1 tablespoon	margarine or butter	2 tablespoons
3 cups	bread flour	4 cups
1 tablespoon	sugar	4 teaspoons
¾ teaspoon	salt	1 teaspoon
1 teaspoon	active dry yeast or bread machine yeast	1¼ teaspoons

Almond extract delicately flavors this loaf, and strained peaches make preparation super simple.

Select the loaf size. Add the ingredients to the machine according to the manufacturer's directions. Select the basic white bread cycle.

*Note: Our Test Kitchen recommends ¼ teaspoon almond extract for either size loaf.

NUTRITION FACTS PER SLICE

		Daily Values
Calories	123	6%
Total fat	2 g	3%
Sat. fat	1 g	4%
Cholesterol	4 mg	1%
Sodium	111 mg	4%
Carbo.	22 g	7%
Fiber	1 g	4%
Protein	3 g	

Applesauce Bread

Bursting with flavor from applesauce, oats, and mace, this loaf has the old-fashioned goodness of Grandmother's favorite recipes.

1½-pound* (20 slices)	Ingredients	2-pound* (27 slices)
¾ cup	water	1 cup
½ cup	applesauce	⅔ cup
1 tablespoon	margarine or butter	4 teaspoons
3 cups	bread flour	4 cups
⅓ cup	old-fashioned or quick-cooking rolled oats	½ cup
1 tablespoon	brown sugar	4 teaspoons
¾ teaspoon	salt	1 teaspoon
¼ teaspoon	ground mace**	¼ teaspoon
1 teaspoon	active dry yeast or bread machine yeast	1¼ teaspoons

NUTRITION FACTS PER SLICE		Daily Values
Calories	92	4%
Total fat	1 g	1%
Sat. fat	0 g	0%
Cholesterol	0 mg	0%
Sodium	88 mg	3%
Carbo.	18 g	5%
Fiber	1 g	3%
Protein	3 g	

Select the loaf size. Add the ingredients to the machine according to the manufacturer's directions. Select the basic white bread cycle.

*Note: For the 1½-pound loaf, the bread machine pan must have a capacity of 10 cups or more. For the 2-pound loaf, the bread machine pan must have a capacity of 12 cups or more.

**Note: Our Test Kitchen recommends ¼ teaspoon ground mace for either size loaf.

Banana-Blueberry Bread

1½-pound* (16 slices)	Ingredients	2-pound* (22 slices)
⅔ cup	buttermilk	¾ cup
½ cup	mashed ripe banana	⅔ cup
1	egg**	1
1 tablespoon	margarine or butter	4 teaspoons
3 cups	bread flour	4 cups
3 tablespoons	sugar	¼ cup
¾ teaspoon	salt	1 teaspoon
1 teaspoon	active dry yeast or bread machine yeast	1¼ teaspoons
⅓ cup	dried blueberries or snipped dried tart red cherries	½ cup

With the help of dried blueberries or cherries, you can make this fragrant banana bread all year long. Look for dried fruits in the produce or dried-fruit section of your supermarket.

Select the loaf size. Add the ingredients to the machine according to the manufacturer's directions. Select the basic white bread cycle.

*Note: For the 1½-pound loaf, the bread machine pan must have a capacity of 10 cups or more. For the 2-pound loaf, the bread machine pan must have a capacity of 12 cups or more.

**Note: Our Test Kitchen recommends 1 egg for either size loaf.

NUTRITION FACTS PER SLICE		Daily Values
Calories	141	7%
Total fat	2 g	2%
Sat. fat	<0.5 g	1%
Cholesterol	14 mg	4%
Sodium	123 mg	5%
Carbo.	27 g	9%
Fiber	1 g	3%
Protein	4 g	

INTERNATIONAL CLASSICS

At left: *Russian Kulich*

ITALIAN CHEESE BREAD

Adapted from a traditional favorite of bakers in the Italian province of Umbria, this loaf gets its flavor from pecorino Romano cheese. This specific variety of Romano is made from sheep's milk and has a sharp and tangy flavor. Look for the cheese at Italian specialty food stores or in larger supermarkets.

1½-pound* (16 slices)	Ingredients	2-pound* (22 slices)
¾ cup	milk	1 cup
3 tablespoons	water	¼ cup
1	egg**	1
1 tablespoon	margarine or butter	4 teaspoons
3 cups	bread flour	4 cups
¾ cup (3 ounces)	finely shredded pecorino Romano or Romano cheese	1 cup (4 ounces)
½ teaspoon	salt	¾ teaspoon
1 teaspoon	active dry yeast or bread machine yeast	1¼ teaspoons

NUTRITION FACTS PER SLICE

		Daily Values
Calories	131	6%
Total fat	3 g	4%
Sat. fat	<0.5 g	2%
Cholesterol	18 mg	5%
Sodium	145 mg	6%
Carbo.	20 g	6%
Fiber	1 g	3%
Protein	6 g	

Select the loaf size. Add the ingredients to the machine according to the manufacturer's directions. Select the basic white bread cycle.

*Note: For the 1½-pound loaf, the bread machine pan must have a capacity of 10 cups or more. For the 2-pound loaf, the bread machine pan must have a capacity of 12 cups or more.

**Note: Our Test Kitchen recommends 1 egg for either size loaf.

ITALIAN WHOLE WHEAT SAGE BREAD

1½-pound (16 slices)	Ingredients	2-pound (22 slices)
1 cup	water	1⅓ cups
1 tablespoon	olive oil or cooking oil	4 teaspoons
2 cups	bread flour	2⅔ cups
1 cup	whole wheat flour	1⅓ cups
1 teaspoon	sugar	1½ teaspoons
2 teaspoons	snipped fresh sage*	1 tablespoon
¾ teaspoon	salt	1 teaspoon
1 teaspoon	active dry yeast or bread machine yeast	1¼ teaspoons

Sage gives this old-world loaf, based on a recipe from the Italian province of Tuscany, a sensational herb flavor.

Select the loaf size. Add the ingredients to the machine according to the manufacturer's directions. If available, select the whole grain cycle, or select the basic white bread cycle.

*Note: If you can't find fresh sage, use ¼ teaspoon dried sage, crushed, for the 1½-pound loaf. Use ½ teaspoon dried sage, crushed, for the 2-pound loaf.

NUTRITION FACTS PER SLICE		
		Daily Values
Calories	97	4%
Total fat	1 g	1%
Sat. fat	0 g	0%
Cholesterol	0 mg	0%
Sodium	101 mg	4%
Carbo.	18 g	6%
Fiber	2 g	6%
Protein	3 g	

GERMAN CARAWAY SEED LOAF

German bakers use caraway seed to add a distinctive flavor to both white and whole grain breads. Serve slices of this loaf with your favorite soup.

1½-pound* (16 slices)	Ingredients	2-pound* (22 slices)
⅓ cup	milk	½ cup
⅓ cup	water	½ cup
1	egg**	1
¼ cup	margarine or butter, cut up	⅓ cup
3 cups	bread flour	4 cups
1½ teaspoons	sugar	2 teaspoons
2 teaspoons	caraway seed	1 tablespoon
¾ teaspoon	salt	1 teaspoon
1 teaspoon	active dry yeast or bread machine yeast	1¼ teaspoons

NUTRITION FACTS PER SLICE		Daily Values
Calories	129	6%
Total fat	4 g	5%
Sat. fat	1 g	3%
Cholesterol	14 mg	4%
Sodium	141 mg	5%
Carbo.	20 g	6%
Fiber	1 g	3%
Protein	4 g	

Select the loaf size. Add the ingredients to the machine according to the manufacturer's directions. Select the basic white bread cycle.

*Note: For the 1½-pound loaf, the bread machine pan must have a capacity of 10 cups or more. For the 2-pound loaf, the bread machine pan must have a capacity of 12 cups or more.

**Note: Our Test Kitchen recommends 1 egg for either size loaf.

SCANDINAVIAN RYE BREAD

1½-pound (16 slices)	Ingredients	2-pound (22 slices)
¾ cup	water	1 cup
¼ cup	dark-colored corn syrup	⅓ cup
1 tablespoon	margarine, butter, or cooking oil	4 teaspoons
2 cups	bread flour	2⅔ cups
1 cup	rye flour	1⅓ cups
2 teaspoons	gluten flour	1 tablespoon
1½ teaspoons	finely shredded orange peel	2 teaspoons
¾ teaspoon	salt	1 teaspoon
½ teaspoon	fennel seed	¾ teaspoon
½ teaspoon	caraway seed	¾ teaspoon
1 teaspoon	active dry yeast or bread machine yeast	1¼ teaspoons

Boasting the triple-flavor combination of orange peel, caraway seed, and fennel seed, this dark rye bread typifies the hearty breads made throughout Scandinavia.

Select the loaf size. Add the ingredients to the machine according to the manufacturer's directions. If available, select the whole grain cycle, or select the basic white bread cycle.

NUTRITION FACTS PER SLICE		
		Daily Values
Calories	109	5%
Total fat	1 g	1%
Sat. fat	0 g	0%
Cholesterol	0 mg	0%
Sodium	113 mg	4%
Carbo.	22 g	7%
Fiber	1 g	5%
Protein	3 g	

FRENCH PEAR BREAD

Inspired by a bread from central France, this deliciously distinctive loaf is sweetened with honey and spiced with just a touch of pepper. Select either juice-packed or syrup-packed canned pears and mash them well before adding.

1½-pound* (20 slices)	Ingredients	2-pound* (27 slices)
¾ cup	mashed canned pears	1 cup
¼ cup	water	⅓ cup
1 tablespoon	honey	4 teaspoons
1	egg**	1
3 cups	bread flour	4 cups
¾ teaspoon	salt	1 teaspoon
⅛ teaspoon	pepper	¼ teaspoon
1 teaspoon	active dry yeast or bread machine yeast	1¼ teaspoons

NUTRITION FACTS PER SLICE		Daily Values
Calories	89	4%
Total fat	1 g	0%
Sat. fat	0 g	0%
Cholesterol	11 mg	3%
Sodium	84 mg	3%
Carbo.	18 g	5%
Fiber	1 g	3%
Protein	3 g	

Select the loaf size. Add the ingredients to the machine according to the manufacturer's directions. Select the basic white bread cycle.

*Note: For the 1½-pound loaf, the bread machine pan must have a capacity of 10 cups or more. For the 2-pound loaf, the bread machine pan must have a capacity of 12 cups or more.

**Note: Our Test Kitchen recommends 1 egg for either size loaf.

RUSSIAN KULICH

1½-pound* (16 slices)	Ingredients	2-pound* (22 slices)
⅓ cup	dark raisins	½ cup
2 tablespoons	orange juice	3 tablespoons
Dash	powdered saffron	Few dashes
¼ cup	milk	⅓ cup
⅓ cup	water	½ cup
1 teaspoon	vanilla	1½ teaspoons
¼ teaspoon	almond extract**	¼ teaspoon
2 tablespoons	margarine or butter, cut up	3 tablespoons
1	egg**	1
3 cups	bread flour	4 cups
2 tablespoons	sugar	3 tablespoons
¾ teaspoon	salt	1 teaspoon
1½ teaspoons	active dry yeast or bread machine yeast	2 teaspoons
⅓ cup	mixed candied fruits and peels	½ cup
	Glaze	

This bread machine adaptation of Russian Easter bread isn't the traditional cylindrical shape, but everything else about it is as authentic as can be. It's brimming with the traditional ingredients: raisins, saffron, and candied fruits and peels. If you like, garnish the top of the glazed bread with additional chopped candied fruits and peels.

Pictured on page 76.

Select the loaf size. Combine first 3 ingredients; let stand 10 minutes. Add mixture and remaining ingredients except Glaze to machine according to manufacturer's directions. Select basic white bread cycle. Drizzle cooled loaf with Glaze.

Glaze: Combine 1 cup sifted *powdered sugar,* few drops *almond extract,* and 1 to 2 tablespoons *milk.*

*Note: For the 1½-pound loaf, the bread machine pan must have a capacity of 10 cups or more. For the 2-pound loaf, the bread machine pan must have a capacity of 12 cups or more.

**Note: Our Test Kitchen recommends ¼ teaspoon almond extract and 1 egg for either size loaf.

NUTRITION FACTS PER SLICE		
		Daily Values
Calories	166	8%
Total fat	2 g	3%
Sat. fat	<0.5 g	2%
Cholesterol	14 mg	4%
Sodium	124 mg	5%
Carbo.	32 g	10%
Fiber	1 g	4%
Protein	4 g	

WELSH CURRANT BREAD

Filled with currants and spiced with cinnamon, allspice, nutmeg, and cloves, this sweet bread lives up to its Welsh name of bara brith, or "speckled loaf."

1½-pound* (16 slices)	Ingredients	2-pound* (22 slices)
¾ cup	buttermilk	1 cup
1	egg**	1
3 tablespoons	margarine or butter, cut up	¼ cup
3 cups	bread flour	4 cups
2 tablespoons	brown sugar	3 tablespoons
¾ teaspoon	salt	1 teaspoon
¾ teaspoon	ground cinnamon	1 teaspoon
⅛ teaspoon	ground allspice	¼ teaspoon
⅛ teaspoon	ground nutmeg	¼ teaspoon
Dash	ground cloves	⅛ teaspoon
1¼ teaspoons	active dry yeast or bread machine yeast	1½ teaspoons
⅔ cup	dried currants	¾ cup
	honey (optional)	

NUTRITION FACTS PER SLICE

		Daily Values
Calories	145	7%
Total fat	3 g	4%
Sat. fat	1 g	3%
Cholesterol	14 mg	4%
Sodium	142 mg	5%
Carbo.	25 g	8%
Fiber	1 g	5%
Protein	4 g	

Select the loaf size. Add all of the ingredients except the honey to the machine according to the manufacturer's directions. Select the basic white bread cycle. If desired, brush the cooled loaf with honey.

*Note: For the 1½-pound loaf, the bread machine pan must have a capacity of 10 cups or more. For the 2-pound loaf, the bread machine pan must have a capacity of 12 cups or more.

**Note: Our Test Kitchen recommends 1 egg for either size loaf.

NORWEGIAN RAISIN-BEER BREAD

1½-pound (16 slices)	Ingredients	2-pound (22 slices)
½ cup	milk	⅔ cup
½ cup	beer	⅔ cup
1 tablespoon	margarine or butter	4 teaspoons
2½ cups	bread flour	3⅓ cups
½ cup	rye flour	⅔ cup
1 tablespoon	gluten flour	4 teaspoons
3 tablespoons	packed brown sugar	¼ cup
¾ teaspoon	salt	1 teaspoon
¼ teaspoon	ground cinnamon	½ teaspoon
¼ teaspoon	ground ginger	½ teaspoon
⅛ teaspoon	pepper	¼ teaspoon
⅛ teaspoon	ground cloves*	⅛ teaspoon
1 teaspoon	active dry yeast or bread machine yeast	1¼ teaspoons
½ cup	dark raisins	⅔ cup

In Norway, bakers add beer to rye bread for a fuller flavor. You can substitute nonalcoholic beer if you prefer.

Select the loaf size. Add the ingredients to the machine according to the manufacturer's directions. Select the basic white bread cycle.

*Note: Our Test Kitchen recommends ⅛ teaspoon ground cloves for either size loaf.

NUTRITION FACTS PER SLICE		Daily Values
Calories	126	6%
Total fat	1 g	2%
Sat. fat	<0.5 g	1%
Cholesterol	1 mg	0%
Sodium	114 mg	4%
Carbo.	25 g	8%
Fiber	1 g	5%
Protein	4 g	

FINNISH CARDAMOM LOAF

*A popular
Scandinavian
spice, cardamom
gives this rich
bread a wonderful
fragrance and a
spicy-sweet flavor.
Try a slice topped
with cream cheese.*

1½-pound* (20 slices)	Ingredients	2-pound* (27 slices)
¾ cup	evaporated milk	1 cup
¼ cup	water**	¼ cup
1	egg**	1
2 tablespoons	margarine or butter, cut up	3 tablespoons
3 cups	bread flour	4 cups
⅓ cup	sugar	½ cup
¾ teaspoon	salt	1 teaspoon
¾ teaspoon	ground cardamom	1 teaspoon
1 teaspoon	active dry yeast or bread machine yeast	1¼ teaspoons

NUTRITION FACTS PER SLICE		
		Daily Values
Calories	115	5%
Total fat	2 g	3%
Sat. fat	1 g	3%
Cholesterol	13 mg	4%
Sodium	107 mg	4%
Carbo.	19 g	6%
Fiber	1 g	2%
Protein	4 g	

Select the loaf size. Add the ingredients to the machine according to the manufacturer's directions. Select the basic white bread cycle. If available, try the light-crust color setting.

*Note: For the 1½-pound loaf, the bread machine pan must have a capacity of 10 cups or more. For the 2-pound loaf, the bread machine pan must have a capacity of 12 cups or more.

**Note: Our Test Kitchen recommends ¼ cup water and 1 egg for either size loaf.

POPPY SEED KOLACKY

1½-pound (12 kolacky)	Ingredients	2-pound (18 kolacky)
½ cup	milk	¾ cup
2	eggs*	2
¼ cup	margarine or butter, cut up	⅓ cup
3 cups	bread flour	4 cups
⅓ cup	sugar	½ cup
¾ teaspoon	salt	1 teaspoon
¾ teaspoon	finely shredded lemon peel	1 teaspoon
1 teaspoon	active dry yeast or bread machine yeast	1¼ teaspoons
	Filling	

In Eastern Europe, these poppy-seed and raisin-filled "pillows" symbolize good luck and prosperity.

Select recipe size. Add all ingredients except Filling to machine according to manufacturer's directions. Select the dough cycle. When cycle is complete, remove dough. Punch down; cover and let rest for 10 minutes. Divide 1½-pound dough into 12 pieces and 2-pound dough into 18 pieces. Shape into balls. On lightly floured surface, roll out balls to 3½-inch-diameter circles. Place 3 inches apart on greased baking sheets. Cover; let rise in warm place 45 to 60 minutes or until double.

With floured thumb, make large depression in center of each circle. Spoon Filling into depressions. Bake in 375° oven for 10 to 12 minutes or until golden. Cool on wire racks.

Filling: Place ¾ cup *golden* or *dark raisins* in a small mixing bowl; pour enough *boiling water* over raisins to cover. Let stand 10 minutes; drain well. Place raisins, ¼ cup *poppy seed,* ¼ cup *honey,* 1 tablespoon *margarine* or *butter,* and ⅛ teaspoon *ground allspice* in a blender container or food processor bowl. Cover; blend or process until nearly smooth. Transfer to a small saucepan. Bring to boiling; reduce heat. Simmer, uncovered, for 2 to 3 minutes or until slightly thickened, stirring often. Cool.

*Note: Our Test Kitchen recommends 2 eggs for either size recipe.

NUTRITION FACTS PER KOLACKY		Daily Values
Calories	274	13%
Total fat	8 g	11%
Sat. fat	2 g	7%
Cholesterol	36 mg	12%
Sodium	207 mg	8%
Carbo.	46 g	15%
Fiber	1 g	5%
Protein	7 g	

FLATBREADS AND PIZZAS

At left: *Rosemary-Fig Focaccia*

ROSEMARY-FIG FOCACCIA

Flecks of almonds, dried figs, and snipped rosemary make this chewy flatbread as visually appealing as it is delicious.

Pictured on page 88.

1½-pound (12 wedges)	Ingredients	2-pound (18 wedges)
¾ cup	water	1 cup
¼ cup	cooking oil	⅓ cup
3 cups	bread flour	4 cups
¾ teaspoon	salt	1 teaspoon
1 teaspoon	active dry yeast or bread machine yeast	1¼ teaspoons
⅓ cup	coarsely chopped almonds	½ cup
¼ cup	coarsely snipped dried figs	⅓ cup
2 teaspoons	snipped fresh rosemary*	2½ teaspoons
	melted margarine or butter (optional)	

NUTRITION FACTS PER WEDGE		
		Daily Values
Calories	194	9%
Total fat	7 g	10%
Sat. fat	1 g	4%
Cholesterol	0 mg	0%
Sodium	137 mg	5%
Carbo.	28 g	9%
Fiber	2 g	7%
Protein	5 g	

Select the recipe size. Add all of the ingredients except the melted margarine or butter to the machine according to the manufacturer's directions. Select the dough cycle. When the cycle is complete, remove dough from machine. Punch down. Cover and let rest for 10 minutes.

Grease an 11- or 12-inch pizza pan. (For the 2-pound recipe, grease a 13- or 14-inch pizza pan.) Place dough on prepared pan. Using the palms of your hands, pat the dough into an even round, just slightly smaller than the pan. Using your fingertips, poke the dough all over to dimple the surface. Cover loosely; let rise in a warm place 30 minutes. Bake in a 400° oven for about 20 minutes or until edge is golden brown. If desired, brush with melted margarine or butter. Serve warm or cool, cut into wedges.

*Note: If you can't find fresh rosemary, use ¾ teaspoon dried rosemary, crushed, for the 1½-pound recipe or 1 teaspoon dried rosemary, crushed, for the 2-pound recipe.

OLIVE FOCACCIA

1½-pound (12 wedges)	Ingredients	2-pound (18 wedges)
¾ cup	water	1 cup
¼ cup	olive oil or cooking oil	⅓ cup
3 cups	bread flour	4 cups
1 teaspoon	sugar	1½ teaspoons
2 tablespoons	snipped fresh savory*	3 tablespoons
¾ teaspoon	salt	1 teaspoon
1 teaspoon	active dry yeast or bread machine yeast	1¼ teaspoons
¼ cup	coarsely chopped pitted ripe olives	⅓ cup
¼ to ⅓ cup	purchased pesto	⅓ to ½ cup

For a flavorful variation, omit the pesto and brush the dough with olive oil, then sprinkle it with snipped fresh basil and finely shredded Parmesan cheese. For the 1½-pound recipe, use 4 teaspoons olive oil and ¼ cup each of basil and Parmesan cheese. For the 2-pound recipe, use 2 tablespoons olive oil and ⅓ cup each of basil and Parmesan cheese.

Select the recipe size. Add all of the ingredients except the pesto to the machine according to the manufacturer's directions. Select the dough cycle. When the cycle is complete, remove dough from machine. Punch down. Cover and let rest for 10 minutes.

Grease an 11- or 12-inch pizza pan. (For the 2-pound recipe, grease a 13- or 14-inch pizza pan.) Place dough on prepared pan. Using the palms of your hands, pat the dough into an even round, just slightly smaller than the pan. Using your fingertips, poke the dough all over to dimple the surface. Spread the pesto over the dough. Cover loosely; let rise in a warm place 30 minutes. Bake in a 400° oven for 25 to 30 minutes or until edge is golden brown. Serve warm or cool, cut into wedges. Store leftovers in the freezer.

*Note: If you can't find fresh savory, use 1½ teaspoons dried savory, crushed, for the 1½-pound recipe or 2 teaspoons dried savory, crushed, for the 2-pound recipe.

NUTRITION FACTS PER WEDGE

		Daily Values
Calories	206	10%
Total fat	9 g	13%
Sat. fat	1 g	3%
Cholesterol	1 mg	0%
Sodium	186 mg	7%
Carbo.	26 g	8%
Fiber	1 g	4%
Protein	5 g	

CARAMELIZED ONION AND WALNUT FOCACCIA

This sophisticated bread is equally tasty as an appetizer or accompaniment for a gourmet meal.

1½-pound (12 wedges)	Ingredients	2-pound (18 wedges)
¾ cup	water	1 cup
¼ cup	cooking oil	⅓ cup
3 cups	bread flour	4 cups
¾ teaspoon	salt	1 teaspoon
1 teaspoon	active dry yeast or bread machine yeast	1¼ teaspoons
2 tablespoons	margarine or butter	3 tablespoons
4 medium (4 cups)	onions, halved and thinly sliced	5 medium (5 cups)
1½ teaspoons	sugar	2 teaspoons
⅓ cup	coarsely chopped walnuts or pine nuts	½ cup

NUTRITION FACTS PER WEDGE		
		Daily Values
Calories	223	11%
Total fat	9 g	14%
Sat. fat	1 g	6%
Cholesterol	0 mg	0%
Sodium	158 mg	6%
Carbo.	30 g	10%
Fiber	2 g	7%
Protein	5 g	

Select the recipe size. Add the first 5 ingredients to the machine according to the manufacturer's directions. Select the dough cycle. When the cycle is complete, remove dough from machine. Punch down. Cover and let rest for 10 minutes.

Grease an 11- or 12-inch pizza pan. (For the 2-pound recipe, grease a 13- or 14-inch pizza pan.) Place dough on prepared pan. Using the palms of your hands, pat the dough into an even round, just slightly smaller than the pan. Using your fingertips, poke the dough all over to dimple the surface. Cover loosely; let rise in a warm place 30 minutes.

Meanwhile, for the topping, in a large saucepan melt the margarine or butter. Add the onions. Cover and cook over medium-low heat for about 15 minutes or until onions are tender and golden brown, stirring occasionally. Sprinkle the sugar over onions. Cook, uncovered, for 10 to 15 minutes more or until browned, stirring occasionally.

Bake the dough in a 425° oven for 7 to 10 minutes or until lightly browned. Spoon onion mixture over; sprinkle with the nuts. Bake for 10 minutes more. Serve warm, cut into wedges. Store leftovers in the freezer.

MULTIGRAIN FLATBREAD

1½-pound (16 servings)	Ingredients
1 cup	buttermilk
¼ cup	water
2 tablespoons	dark-colored corn syrup
1½ cups	bread flour
¾ cup	whole wheat flour
¾ cup	rye flour
¾ teaspoon	salt
½ teaspoon	caraway seed
¼ teaspoon	aniseed (optional)
1 teaspoon	active dry yeast or bread machine yeast
	milk or buttermilk

Make this dough 1½ pounds at a time; bigger batches will rise too much before they're baked.

Add all of the ingredients except the milk or buttermilk to the machine according to the manufacturer's directions. Select the dough cycle. When the cycle is complete, remove dough from machine. Punch dough down. Cover; let rest for 10 minutes.

Grease 2 large baking sheets or 12-inch pizza pans. Divide dough into fourths. Cover and refrigerate 2 portions of the dough. On a lightly floured surface, roll each of the remaining portions into a 12-inch circle. Transfer to prepared baking sheets or pizza pans.

Using a fork, prick the entire surface of each round several times. Brush rounds with milk or buttermilk. Bake in a 400° oven for 11 to 13 minutes or until crisp and browned, rotating baking sheets halfway through baking. Cool on wire racks. Repeat with remaining portions of dough. Serve warm or cool. Store in an airtight container to maintain crispness.

NUTRITION FACTS PER SERVING		Daily Values
Calories	98	4%
Total fat	1 g	0%
Sat. fat	0 g	0%
Cholesterol	1 mg	0%
Sodium	119 mg	4%
Carbo.	20 g	6%
Fiber	2 g	6%
Protein	3 g	

JALAPEÑO-CHEDDAR ROUNDS

For extra "heat," use finely shredded Monterey Jack cheese with jalapeño peppers instead of the cheddar cheese.

1½-pound (12 wedges)	Ingredients	2-pound (16 wedges)
¾ cup	milk	1 cup
2 tablespoons	olive oil or cooking oil	3 tablespoons
3 cups	bread flour	4 cups
2 teaspoons	sugar	1 tablespoon
1 small	fresh jalapeño pepper, seeded and finely chopped*	1 medium
¾ teaspoon	salt	1 teaspoon
1 teaspoon	active dry yeast or bread machine yeast	1¼ teaspoons
½ cup	finely shredded cheddar cheese	⅔ cup

NUTRITION FACTS
PER WEDGE

		Daily Values
Calories	174	8%
Total fat	5 g	7%
Sat. fat	2 g	7%
Cholesterol	6 mg	2%
Sodium	171 mg	7%
Carbo.	27 g	8%
Fiber	1 g	4%
Protein	6 g	

Select the recipe size. Add all of the ingredients except the cheddar cheese to the machine according to the manufacturer's directions. Select the dough cycle. When the cycle is complete, remove dough from machine. Punch down. Cover and let rest for 10 minutes.

Grease large baking sheets. Divide 1½-pound dough into thirds or divide 2-pound dough into quarters. On a lightly floured surface, pat or roll each portion of dough into an even round about 7 inches in diameter. Transfer rounds to the prepared baking sheets. Using your fingertips, poke the dough all over to dimple the surface. Cover loosely; let rise in a warm place 30 minutes.

Sprinkle cheddar cheese evenly over rounds. Bake in a 400° oven for about 20 minutes or until edges are golden brown. Serve warm or cool, cut into wedges. Store leftovers in the freezer.

*Note: Protect your hands when working with hot peppers by wearing plastic or rubber gloves, or working with plastic bags on your hands. If your bare hands touch the peppers, wash your hands and under your nails thoroughly with soap and water. Avoid rubbing your mouth, nose, eyes, or ears when working with hot peppers.

CINNAMON-SUGAR ROUNDS

1½-pound (12 wedges)	Ingredients	2-pound (16 wedges)
¾ cup	milk	1 cup
1	egg*	1
¼ cup	margarine or butter, cut up	⅓ cup
3 cups	bread flour	4 cups
1 tablespoon	sugar	4 teaspoons
¾ teaspoon	salt	1 teaspoon
1 teaspoon	active dry yeast or bread machine yeast	1¼ teaspoons
3 tablespoons	coarse sugar	¼ cup
1 teaspoon	ground cinnamon	1¼ teaspoons
1 tablespoon	margarine or butter, melted	4 teaspoons

Sweet and spicy, these tender rounds make tasty after-school snacks. Look for coarse or decorating sugar where cake and cookie decorating supplies are sold.

Select the recipe size. Add the first 7 ingredients to the machine according to the manufacturer's directions. Select the dough cycle. When the cycle is complete, remove dough from machine. Punch down. Cover and let rest for 10 minutes.

Grease large baking sheets. Divide 1½-pound dough into thirds or divide 2-pound dough into quarters. On a lightly floured surface, using the palms of your hands, pat each portion of dough into an even round about 7 inches in diameter. Transfer rounds to prepared baking sheets. Using your fingertips, poke the dough all over to dimple the surface. Cover loosely; let rise in a warm place for 30 minutes.

In a small mixing bowl stir together the coarse sugar and cinnamon. Brush melted margarine or butter evenly over rounds; sprinkle with sugar-cinnamon mixture. Bake in a 350° oven for 15 to 20 minutes or until edges are golden brown. Serve warm or cool, cut into wedges.

*Note: Our Test Kitchen recommends 1 egg for either size recipe.

NUTRITION FACTS PER WEDGE

		Daily Values
Calories	198	9%
Total fat	6 g	9%
Sat. fat	1 g	6%
Cholesterol	19 mg	6%
Sodium	203 mg	8%
Carbo.	30 g	10%
Fiber	1 g	4%
Protein	5 g	

PIZZA DOUGH

Top this versatile pizza crust with your favorite flavors or try one of these savory combinations: 1) purchased Alfredo sauce, dried tomatoes, cooked chicken, and mozzarella cheese; 2) red onions, tomatoes, cooked artichoke hearts, and Swiss cheese; 3) cooked shrimp, ripe olives, green onions, and semisoft cheese with herbs.

1½-pound* (6 servings)	Ingredients	2-pound* (9 servings)
1 cup	water	1⅓ cups
4 teaspoons	olive oil or cooking oil	2 tablespoons
3 cups	bread flour	4 cups
¾ teaspoon	salt	1 teaspoon
1 teaspoon	active dry yeast or bread machine yeast	1¼ teaspoons
	cornmeal (optional)	

Select the recipe size. Add all of the ingredients except cornmeal to the machine according to the manufacturer's directions. Select the dough cycle. When the cycle is complete, remove dough from machine. Punch down. Cover and let rest 10 minutes. Make thin-crust or thick-crust pizza (see directions on page 97).

*Note: The 1½-pound recipe makes two 11- or 12-inch thin-crust pizzas or one 13- or 14-inch thick-crust pizza. The 2-pound recipe makes two 13- or 14-inch thin-crust pizzas or two 13×9-inch thick-crust pizzas.

NUTRITION FACTS PER
SERVING WITHOUT TOPPINGS

		Daily Values
Calories	276	13%
Total fat	4 g	6%
Sat. fat	1 g	2%
Cholesterol	0 mg	0%
Sodium	269 mg	11%
Carbo.	50 g	16%
Fiber	2 g	8%
Protein	8 g	

SHAPING PIZZA DOUGH

You can make thin-crust or thick-crust pizza from the pizza doughs on pages 96, 98, and 99. Just shape and bake as directed below.

For thin-crust pizza using the 1½-pound recipe, divide dough in half. *For each pizza, grease an* 11- or 12-inch pizza pan or a large baking sheet. If desired, sprinkle pan with cornmeal. On lightly floured surface, roll 1 portion of dough into a 12- to 13-inch circle. Transfer to prepared pan, building up edge slightly. Prick crust with a fork. Do not let dough rise. Bake in a 425° oven 10 to 12 minutes or until lightly browned. Add desired topping. Bake for 10 to 15 minutes more or until edge of crust is golden brown and the topping is bubbly.

For thin-crust pizza using the 2-pound recipe, divide dough in half. *For each pizza, grease a* 13- or 14-inch pizza pan or a large baking sheet. If desired, sprinkle greased pan with cornmeal. On a lightly floured surface, roll 1 portion of the dough into a 14- to 15-inch circle. Transfer to the prepared pan, building up edge slightly. Prick crust with a fork. Do not let dough rise. Bake in a 425° oven for 10 to

12 minutes or until lightly browned. Add desired topping. Bake for 10 to 15 minutes more or until the edge of the crust is golden brown and the topping is bubbly.

For thick-crust pizza using the 1½-pound recipe, grease a 13- or 14-inch pizza pan. If desired, sprinkle greased pan with cornmeal. With greased fingers, pat dough into prepared pan, building up the edge. Cover and let rise in a warm place for 30 to 45 minutes or until nearly double. Bake in a 375° oven for 20 to 25 minutes or until lightly browned. Add desired topping. Bake for 15 to 20 minutes more or until the topping is bubbly.

For thick-crust pizza using the 2-pound recipe, divide dough in half. *For each pizza, grease a* 13×9×2-inch baking pan. If desired, sprinkle greased pan with cornmeal. With greased fingers, pat dough into prepared pan, building up the edge. Cover and let rise in a warm place for 30 to 45 minutes or until nearly double. Bake in a 375° oven for 20 to 25 minutes or until lightly browned. Add desired topping. Bake for 15 to 20 minutes more or until the topping is bubbly.

To freeze extra pizza dough, wrap it in plastic wrap and place it in a freezer bag. Seal, label, and freeze the dough for up to 3 months. To thaw, let the dough stand at room temperature for about 2½ hours. Or, thaw it overnight in the refrigerator.

HERBED WHOLE WHEAT PIZZA DOUGH

This herb-seasoned crust blends well with any one of these topping ideas: 1) cream cheese, zucchini, roasted red peppers, and green onions; 2) purchased Alfredo sauce, mushrooms, green onions, and Monterey Jack cheese; 3) chunky pizza sauce, ham, onions, and cheddar cheese.

1½-pound* (6 servings)	Ingredients	2-pound* (9 servings)
1 cup	water	1⅓ cups
2 tablespoons	olive oil or cooking oil	3 tablespoons
2 cups	bread flour	2⅔ cups
1 cup	whole wheat flour	1⅓ cups
2 teaspoons	dried basil, oregano, or Italian seasoning, crushed	1 tablespoon
¾ teaspoon	salt	1 teaspoon
¼ teaspoon	garlic powder	½ teaspoon
1 teaspoon	active dry yeast or bread machine yeast	1¼ teaspoons
	cornmeal (optional)	

NUTRITION FACTS PER SERVING WITHOUT TOPPINGS		
		Daily Values
Calories	276	13%
Total fat	6 g	8%
Sat. fat	1 g	3%
Cholesterol	0 mg	0%
Sodium	269 mg	11%
Carbo.	48 g	16%
Fiber	4 g	16%
Protein	9 g	

Select the recipe size. Add all of the ingredients except cornmeal to the machine according to the manufacturer's directions. Select the dough cycle. When the cycle is complete, remove dough from machine. Punch down. Cover and let rest 10 minutes. Make thin-crust or thick-crust pizza (see directions on page 97).

*Note: The 1½-pound recipe makes two 11- or 12-inch thin-crust pizzas or one 13- or 14-inch thick-crust pizza. The 2-pound recipe makes two 13- or 14-inch thin-crust pizzas or two 13×9-inch thick-crust pizzas.

CORNMEAL-PARMESAN PIZZA DOUGH

1½-pound* (6 servings)	Ingredients	2-pound* (9 servings)
1 cup	water	1⅓ cups
2 tablespoons	olive oil or cooking oil	3 tablespoons
2½ cups	bread flour	3⅓ cups
½ cup	cornmeal	⅔ cup
½ cup	grated Parmesan cheese	⅔ cup
¾ teaspoon	salt	1 teaspoon
1 teaspoon	active dry yeast or bread machine yeast	1¼ teaspoons
	cornmeal (optional)	

The robust flavor of Parmesan cheese and subtle flavor of cornmeal make this crust ideal for both Mexican- and Italian-style toppings such as: 1) refried beans, salsa, sweet pepper, and Cojack or colby cheese; 2) plum tomatoes, fresh basil, sweet pepper, and mozzarella cheese; 3) pizza sauce, mushrooms, Canadian-style bacon, and pepper cheese.

Select the recipe size. Add all of the ingredients except cornmeal to the machine according to the manufacturer's directions. Select the dough cycle. When the cycle is complete, remove dough from machine. Punch down. Cover and let rest 10 minutes. Make thin-crust or thick-crust pizza (see directions on page 97).

*Note: The 1½-pound recipe makes two 11- or 12-inch thin-crust pizzas or one 13- or 14-inch thick-crust pizza. The 2-pound recipe makes two 13- or 14-inch thin-crust pizzas or two 13×9-inch thick-crust pizzas.

NUTRITION FACTS PER
SERVING WITHOUT TOPPINGS

		Daily Values
Calories	328	16%
Total fat	8 g	12%
Sat. fat	2 g	11%
Cholesterol	7 mg	2%
Sodium	424 mg	17%
Carbo.	51 g	16%
Fiber	2 g	9%
Protein	12 g	

SHAPED BREADS AND ROLLS

At left: *Cranberry-Peach Crescent*

PINE NUT ROLLS

Pine nuts, also known as piñon, pignoli, and pignolia, are cream-colored with a rich, nutty flavor. If they're not available at your supermarket, look for them in Italian markets, Oriental food stores, or health-food stores.

Pictured on page 1.

1½-pound (18 rolls)	Ingredients	2-pound (24 rolls)
⅔ cup	milk	¾ cup
1 tablespoon	honey	4 teaspoons
1	egg(s)	2
3 tablespoons	margarine or butter, cut up	¼ cup
3 cups	bread flour	4 cups
¾ teaspoon	salt	1 teaspoon
1 teaspoon	active dry yeast or bread machine yeast	1¼ teaspoons
⅔ cup	finely chopped pine nuts or almonds	¾ cup
½ cup	grated Parmesan cheese	⅔ cup
⅓ cup	snipped parsley	½ cup
3 tablespoons	margarine or butter, melted	¼ cup
1	egg white*	1
1 tablespoon	water*	1 tablespoon

NUTRITION FACTS PER ROLL

		Daily Values
Calories	174	8%
Total fat	9 g	13%
Sat. fat	2 g	9%
Cholesterol	15 mg	4%
Sodium	197 mg	8%
Carbo.	19 g	6%
Fiber	1 g	2%
Protein	6 g	

Select the recipe size. Add the first 7 ingredients to the machine according to the manufacturer's directions. Select the dough cycle. When the cycle is complete, remove dough from machine. Punch down. Cover and let rest for 10 minutes.

Meanwhile, for filling, in a small mixing bowl stir together pine nuts or almonds, Parmesan cheese, and parsley. Set aside.

For the 1½-pound recipe, grease baking sheets. Divide dough in half. On a lightly floured surface, roll half of the dough into a 13½×12-inch rectangle. Brush with half of the melted margarine or butter; sprinkle with half of the filling. Starting from a long side, roll up jelly-roll style; seal edge. Cut into nine 1½-inch-thick slices. Place slices, seams down, on prepared baking sheets. Let rest 5 minutes. Using a wooden spoon handle, press center of each slice lengthwise to make a deep crease. Repeat with remaining dough, remaining melted margarine or butter, and remaining filling. In a small mixing bowl stir together the egg white and water; brush onto rolls. Let rise in a warm place about 30 minutes or until nearly double. Bake in a 375° oven for about 15 minutes or until golden brown. Serve warm.

For the 2-pound recipe, grease baking sheets. Divide dough in half. On a lightly floured surface, roll half of the dough into an 18×12-inch rectangle. Brush with half of the melted margarine or butter; sprinkle with half of the filling. Starting from a long side, roll up jelly-roll style; seal edge. Cut into twelve 1½-inch-thick slices. Place slices, seams down, on prepared baking sheets. Let rest for 5 minutes. Using a wooden spoon handle, press center of each slice lengthwise to make a deep crease. Repeat with remaining dough, remaining melted margarine or butter, and remaining filling. In a small mixing bowl stir together the egg white and water; brush onto rolls. Let rise in a warm place about 30 minutes or until nearly double. Bake in a 375° oven for about 15 minutes or until golden brown. Serve warm.

*Note: Our Test Kitchen recommends 1 egg white and 1 tablespoon water for either size recipe.

WHEAT CLOVERLEAF ROLLS

Impress your guests with these tangy, easily shaped rolls at your next dinner party. For an extra-special touch, serve them with butter curls, cut ¼-inch-thick slices of butter into shapes with a canapé cutter, or press softened butter into small candy or mint molds and chill until firm.

Pictured on page 1.

1½-pound (16 rolls)	Ingredients	2-pound (24 rolls)
¾ cup	buttermilk	1 cup
1	egg(s)	2
¼ cup	margarine or butter, cut up	⅓ cup
1½ cups	bread flour	2¼ cups
1½ cups	whole wheat flour	2 cups
2 tablespoons	sugar	3 tablespoons
¾ teaspoon	salt	1 teaspoon
1 teaspoon	active dry yeast or bread machine yeast	1¼ teaspoons
1	egg white*	1
1 tablespoon	water*	1 tablespoon
sesame seed, poppy seed, and/or caraway seed		

NUTRITION FACTS PER ROLL		Daily Values
Calories	129	6%
Total fat	4 g	5%
Sat. fat	1 g	3%
Cholesterol	14 mg	4%
Sodium	154 mg	6%
Carbo.	20 g	6%
Fiber	2 g	7%
Protein	4 g	

Select the recipe size. Add the first 8 ingredients to the machine according to the manufacturer's directions. Select the dough cycle. When the cycle is complete, remove dough from machine. Punch down. Cover and let rest for 10 minutes.

For the 1½-pound recipe, lightly grease 16 muffin cups. Divide dough in half. Divide each half into 24 pieces (for a total of 48 pieces). Shape each piece into a ball. Place 3 balls in each muffin cup. In a small mixing bowl stir together the egg white and the water; brush over rolls. Sprinkle rolls lightly with sesame seed, poppy seed, and/or caraway seed. Cover and let rise in a warm place for 20 to 25 minutes or until nearly double. Bake in a 375° oven for 12 to 15 minutes or until golden brown. Serve warm.

For the 2-pound recipe, lightly grease 24 muffin cups. Divide dough in half. Divide each half into 36 pieces (for a total of 72 pieces). Shape each piece into a ball. Place 3 balls in each muffin cup. In a small mixing bowl stir together the egg white and the water; brush over rolls. Sprinkle rolls lightly with sesame seed, poppy seed, and/or caraway seed. Cover; let rise in a warm place for 20 to 25 minutes or until nearly double. Bake in a 375° oven for 12 to 15 minutes or until golden brown. Serve warm.

*Note: Our Test Kitchen recommends 1 egg white and 1 tablespoon water for either size recipe.

PEANUT BUTTER TWISTS

The sweet peanut butter concoction filling these twists often bubbles out while baking. For quick cleanup, line your baking sheets with foil to catch the drips.

1½-pound (24 twists)	Ingredients	2-pound (32 twists)
¾ cup	water	1 cup
1	egg*	1
⅓ cup	margarine or butter, cut up	½ cup
3 cups	bread flour	4 cups
¼ cup	nonfat dry milk powder	⅓ cup
⅓ cup	sugar	½ cup
¾ teaspoon	salt	1 teaspoon
1 teaspoon	active dry yeast or bread machine yeast	1¼ teaspoons
¾ cup	creamy peanut butter	1 cup
⅓ cup	sifted powdered sugar	½ cup
¼ cup	margarine or butter, softened	⅓ cup
	Peanut Butter Icing	
3 tablespoons	chopped peanuts	¼ cup

NUTRITION FACTS PER TWIST

		Daily Values
Calories	209	10%
Total fat	10 g	15%
Sat. fat	2 g	9%
Cholesterol	9 mg	3%
Sodium	180 mg	26%
Carbo.	26 g	8%
Fiber	1 g	4%
Protein	5 g	

Select the recipe size. Add the first 8 ingredients to the machine according to the manufacturer's directions. Select the dough cycle. When the cycle is complete, remove dough from machine. Punch down. Cover and let rest for 10 minutes.

Meanwhile, for filling, in a small mixing bowl combine peanut butter, powdered sugar, and softened margarine or butter. Stir until smooth and spreadable. Set aside.

For the 1½-pound recipe, line 2 baking sheets with foil; lightly grease foil. On a lightly floured surface, roll the dough to a 24×8-inch rectangle; spread with the filling. Fold in half lengthwise; cut crosswise into 24 equal pieces. (If filling oozes out a lot when you make the first cut, cover and chill dough for 15 to 20 minutes, then continue slicing.) Holding both ends of 1 piece, twist; pinch firmly. Place on a prepared baking sheet, pressing ends down. Repeat with remaining pieces. Bake in a 350° oven for 15 minutes or until golden brown. Transfer to wire racks. Drizzle twists with Peanut Butter Icing. Sprinkle peanuts over icing. Serve warm or let cool completely.

For the 2-pound recipe, line a large baking sheet with foil; lightly grease foil. Divide the dough in half; place 1 half in the refrigerator. On a lightly floured surface, roll the remaining half to a 16×9-inch rectangle; spread with half of the filling. Fold in half lengthwise; cut crosswise into 16 equal pieces. (If filling oozes out a lot when you make the first cut, cover and chill dough for 15 to 20 minutes, then continue slicing.) Holding both ends of 1 piece, twist; pinch firmly. Place on prepared baking sheet, pressing ends down. Repeat with remaining cut pieces. Bake in a 350° oven for 15 minutes or until golden brown. Transfer to wire racks. Repeat with chilled half of dough and filling; line baking sheet with new foil. Drizzle twists with Peanut Butter Icing. Sprinkle peanuts over icing. Serve warm or let cool completely.

Peanut Butter Icing: In a medium mixing bowl stir together 1½ cups sifted *powdered sugar* and 2 tablespoons *creamy peanut butter.* Stir in enough *warm water* (2 to 3 tablespoons) to make glaze of drizzling consistency.

*Note: Our Test Kitchen recommends 1 egg for either size recipe.

CRANBERRY-PEACH CRESCENT

To freeze a baked crescent, wrap it in moistureproof and vaporproof freezer wrap and tuck in the freezer for up to 2 months.

Pictured on page 100.

1½-pound (12 servings)	Ingredients	2-pound (16 servings)
½ cup	milk	⅔ cup
¼ cup	water	⅓ cup
1	egg*	1
½ cup	margarine or butter, cut up	⅔ cup
3 cups	bread flour	4 cups
3 tablespoons	sugar	¼ cup
¾ teaspoon	salt	1 teaspoon
1 teaspoon	active dry yeast or bread machine yeast	1¼ teaspoons
¾ cup	cranberries	1 cup
2 tablespoons	sugar	3 tablespoons
2 tablespoons	water	3 tablespoons
1 tablespoon	cold water	4 teaspoons
1 tablespoon	cornstarch	4 teaspoons
¼ cup	peach preserves	⅓ cup
	milk	
	sugar or powdered sugar	

NUTRITION FACTS PER SERVING

		Daily Values
Calories	251	12%
Total fat	9 g	13%
Sat. fat	2 g	8%
Cholesterol	19 mg	6%
Sodium	235 mg	9%
Carbo.	38 g	12%
Fiber	1 g	5%
Protein	5 g	

Select the recipe size. Add the first 8 ingredients to the machine according to the manufacturer's directions. Select the dough cycle. When the cycle is complete, remove dough from machine. Punch down. Cover and let rest for 10 minutes.

Meanwhile, for filling, in a small saucepan combine the cranberries, the 2 or 3 tablespoons sugar, and the 2 or 3 tablespoons water. Bring to boiling; reduce heat. Cook, stirring often, for 3 to 4 minutes or until cranberry skins pop and mixture thickens slightly. Stir together the cold water and cornstarch; stir into cranberry mixture. Cook and stir until the mixture is very thick and just begins to bubble. Remove from heat; stir in preserves. Cover surface with plastic wrap and set aside to cool.

For the 1½-pound recipe, grease a baking sheet. On a lightly floured surface, roll the dough into an 18×10-inch rectangle. Spread the filling down the center of dough in a 3-inch-wide strip. Using a sharp knife, slit dough at 1-inch intervals along each side of filling, cutting from edge of filling to edge of dough. Fold 1 dough strip diagonally over filling and lay down; fold a dough strip from opposite side diagonally over filling, overlapping end of first dough strip. Repeat with remaining dough strips, alternating from side to side and overlapping ends of dough strips. Curve ends to form a crescent shape; carefully transfer to the prepared baking sheet. Cover; let rise in a warm place for 40 to 50 minutes or until nearly double. Bake in a 375° oven for 20 to 25 minutes or until golden brown. (If necessary to prevent overbrowning, cover loosely with foil the last 5 to 10 minutes of baking.) Lightly brush bread with milk and sprinkle with sugar. Or, cool bread completely and sprinkle with powdered sugar.

For the 2-pound recipe, grease 2 baking sheets. Divide the dough in half. On a lightly floured surface, roll half of the dough into a 12×10-inch rectangle. Spread half of the filling lengthwise down the center of the dough in a 3-inch-wide strip. Using a sharp knife, slit dough at 1-inch intervals along each side of filling, cutting from edge of filling to edge of dough. Fold 1 dough strip diagonally over filling and lay down; fold a dough strip from opposite side diagonally over filling, overlapping end of first dough strip. Repeat with remaining dough strips, alternating from side to side and overlapping ends of dough strips. Curve ends to form a crescent shape; carefully transfer to the prepared baking sheet. Repeat with remaining half of dough and remaining filling. Cover; let rise in a warm place for 40 to 50 minutes or until nearly double. Bake in a 375° oven for 20 to 25 minutes or until golden brown. (If necessary to prevent overbrowning, cover loosely with foil the last 5 to 10 minutes of baking.) Lightly brush breads with milk and sprinkle with sugar. Or, cool breads completely and sprinkle with powdered sugar.

*Note: Our Test Kitchen recommends 1 egg for either size recipe.

CHERRY-ALMOND WREATHS

For simple variations, use walnuts or pecans in place of the almonds, or replace the glaze's almond extract with vanilla.

1½-pound (12 servings)	Ingredients	2-pound (16 servings)
¾ cup	milk	1 cup
1	egg*	1
2 tablespoons	margarine or butter, cut up	3 tablespoons
3 cups	bread flour	4 cups
3 tablespoons	sugar	¼ cup
¾ teaspoon	salt	1 teaspoon
¾ teaspoon	ground cinnamon	1 teaspoon
⅛ teaspoon	ground nutmeg	¼ teaspoon
1¼ teaspoons	active dry yeast or bread machine yeast	1½ teaspoons
¾ cup	snipped dried tart cherries	1 cup
⅓ cup	chopped toasted almonds	½ cup
	milk	
	Almond Glaze	
	slivered almonds, toasted	

NUTRITION FACTS
PER SERVING

		Daily Values
Calories	238	11%
Total fat	6 g	8%
Sat. fat	1 g	5%
Cholesterol	19 mg	6%
Sodium	173 mg	7%
Carbo.	40 g	13%
Fiber	2 g	7%
Protein	7 g	

Select the recipe size. Add the first 11 ingredients to the machine according to the manufacturer's directions. Select the dough cycle. When the cycle is complete, remove dough from machine. Punch down. Cover and let rest for 10 minutes.

For the 1½-pound recipe, lightly grease a baking sheet. Divide dough in half. Shape each half into a ball. Roll each ball into an evenly thick rope 25 inches long. Lay the 2 ropes side by side and 1 inch apart; loop 1 rope over the other and twist together loosely. Attach ends to form a circle. Transfer to prepared baking sheet. Cover; let rise in a warm place about 45 minutes or until nearly double. Brush with milk. Bake in a 350° oven for 20 to 30 minutes or until golden brown. Cool on wire racks. Drizzle with the Almond Glaze. Sprinkle with toasted slivered almonds.

For the 2-pound recipe, lightly grease 2 baking sheets. Divide dough into fourths. Shape each fourth into a ball. Roll each ball into an evenly thick rope 20 inches long. Lay 2 of the ropes side by side and 1 inch apart; loop 1 rope over the other and twist together loosely. Attach ends to form a circle. Transfer to a prepared baking sheet. Repeat with the remaining 2 ropes. Cover; let rise in a warm place about 45 minutes or until nearly double. Brush with milk. Bake in a 350° oven for 20 to 30 minutes or until golden brown. Cool wreaths on wire racks. Drizzle wreaths with the Almond Glaze. Sprinkle with toasted slivered almonds.

Almond Glaze: In a small mixing bowl stir together ½ cup sifted *powdered sugar*, 1 teaspoon *margarine* or *butter,* melted, and ¼ teaspoon *almond extract*. Stir in enough *milk* (1 to 2 teaspoons) to make of drizzling consistency.

*Note: Our Test Kitchen recommends 1 egg for either size recipe.

BLUEBERRY TEA RING

Dried blueberries and a cinnamon and brown sugar streusel make an exquisite filling for this rich dough.

1½-pound (16 servings)	Ingredients	2-pound (24 servings)
¾ cup	milk	1 cup
¼ cup	water	⅓ cup
1	egg*	1
¼ cup	margarine or butter, cut up	⅓ cup
3½ cups	bread flour	4⅔ cups
¼ cup	granulated sugar	⅓ cup
¾ teaspoon	salt	1 teaspoon
1 teaspoon	active dry yeast or bread machine yeast	1¼ teaspoons
⅓ cup	packed brown sugar	½ cup
3 tablespoons	bread flour	¼ cup
1 teaspoon	ground cinnamon	1¼ teaspoons
3 tablespoons	margarine or butter	¼ cup
¾ cup	water	1 cup
½ cup	dried blueberries	⅔ cup
	Almond Glaze	

Select the recipe size. Add the first 8 ingredients to the machine according to the manufacturer's directions. Select the dough cycle. When the cycle is complete, remove dough from machine. Punch down. Cover and let rest for 10 minutes.

Meanwhile, for filling, in small mixing bowl stir together the brown sugar, 3 tablespoons or ¼ cup flour,

and the ground cinnamon. With pastry blender or fork, cut in 3 tablespoons or ¼ cup margarine or butter until crumbly. Set aside.

In small saucepan bring ¾ or 1 cup water to boiling; remove from heat. Add the dried blueberries; let stand for 5 minutes. Drain blueberries; pat dry with paper towels. Set aside.

For the 1½-pound recipe, grease a baking sheet. On a lightly floured surface, roll the dough into a 15×9-inch rectangle. Sprinkle filling evenly over dough. Sprinkle with the blueberries. Starting from a long side, roll up jelly-roll style; seal edge. Transfer to the prepared baking sheet, seam side down. Attach ends together to form a circle; pinch seam to seal. Using kitchen scissors or a sharp knife, cut a slit from the outside of dough to center, leaving about 1 inch still attached at the center. Repeat at 1-inch intervals around the ring. Gently turn each slice so 1 of the cut sides faces up. Cover; let rise in a warm place for 45 to 60 minutes or until nearly double. Bake in a 350° oven 30 to 35 minutes or until bread sounds hollow when lightly tapped (the center may be lighter in color). (If necessary to prevent overbrowning, cover loosely with foil the last 5 to 10 minutes of baking.) Cool on a wire rack. Drizzle with Almond Glaze.

For 2-pound recipe, grease a large baking sheet. On a lightly floured surface, roll the dough into an 18×10-inch rectangle. Sprinkle the filling evenly over dough. Sprinkle with blueberries. Starting from a long side, roll up jelly-roll style; seal edge. Transfer to the prepared baking sheet, seam side down. Attach ends together to form a circle; pinch seam to seal. Using kitchen scissors or a sharp knife, cut a slit from the outside of dough to center, leaving about 1 inch still attached at the center. Repeat at 1-inch intervals around the ring. Gently turn each slice so 1 of the cut sides faces up. Cover; let rise in a warm place for 45 to 60 minutes or until nearly double. Bake in a 350° oven about 30 minutes or until the bread sounds hollow when lightly tapped (the center may be lighter in color). (If necessary to prevent overbrowning, cover loosely with foil the last 5 to 10 minutes of baking.) Cool on a wire rack. Drizzle with Almond Glaze.

Almond Glaze: In a small mixing bowl stir together 1¼ cups sifted *powdered sugar,* 1 teaspoon *light-colored corn syrup,* ½ teaspoon *vanilla,* and ¼ teaspoon *almond extract.* Stir in enough *milk* (1 to 2 tablespoons) to make glaze of drizzling consistency.

*Note: Our Test Kitchen recommends 1 egg for either size recipe.

CANDIED FRUIT RING

Packed with red and green cherries, this festive coffee cake makes a colorful centerpiece for a holiday brunch buffet.

1½-pound (16 servings)	Ingredients	2-pound (20 servings)
⅓ cup	orange juice	½ cup
¼ cup	water	⅓ cup
1	egg*	1
3 tablespoons	margarine or butter, cut up	¼ cup
3 cups	bread flour	4 cups
⅓ cup	packed brown sugar	½ cup
¾ teaspoon	salt	1 teaspoon
1¾ teaspoons	active dry yeast or bread machine yeast	2¼ teaspoons
1	egg white*	1
⅓ cup	granulated sugar	½ cup
½ teaspoon	ground cardamom	¾ teaspoon
¾ cup	finely chopped pecans	1 cup
½ cup	finely chopped red and green candied cherries	¾ cup
	Vanilla Glaze	

NUTRITION FACTS PER SERVING		Daily Values
Calories	227	11%
Total fat	6 g	9%
Sat. fat	1 g	4%
Cholesterol	13 mg	4%
Sodium	135 mg	5%
Carbo.	39 g	12%
Fiber	1 g	5%
Protein	4 g	

Select the recipe size. Add the first 8 ingredients to the machine according to the manufacturer's directions. Select the dough cycle. When the cycle is complete, remove dough from machine. Punch down. Cover and let rest for 10 minutes.

Meanwhile, for filling, in a medium mixing bowl beat egg white slightly. Stir in the granulated sugar and cardamom. Then stir in the pecans and cherries. Set aside.

For the 1½-pound recipe, grease a baking sheet. On a lightly floured surface, roll the dough into an 18×12-inch rectangle. Spoon filling over dough. Starting from a long side, roll up jelly-roll style; seal edge. Transfer to the prepared baking sheet, seam side down. Attach ends together to form a ring; pinch seam to seal. Cut slits in a decorative pattern about 1 inch apart around top of ring. Cover; let rise in a warm place for 45 to 60 minutes or u.til nearly double. Bake in a 350° oven for 30 to 35 minutes or until golden brown. Cool on a wire rack. Drizzle with the Vanilla Glaze.

For the 2-pound recipe, grease 2 baking sheets. Divide dough in half. On a lightly floured surface, roll half of the dough into a 16×8-inch rectangle. Spoon half of the filling over dough. Starting from a long side, roll up jelly-roll style; seal edge. Transfer to a prepared baking sheet, seam side down. Attach ends together to form a ring; pinch seam to seal. Cut slits in a decorative pattern about 1 inch apart around top of ring. Repeat with remaining half of dough and remaining filling. Cover; let rise in a warm place for 45 to 60 minutes or until nearly double. Bake in a 350° oven 30 to 35 minutes or until golden brown. Cool on wire racks. Drizzle with the Vanilla Glaze.

Vanilla Glaze: In a small mixing bowl stir together 1 cup sifted *powdered sugar* and ½ teaspoon *vanilla.* Stir in enough *milk* (3 to 4 teaspoons) to make glaze of drizzling consistency.

*Note: Our Test Kitchen recommends 1 egg and 1 egg white for either size recipe.

WALNUT SWIRL BREAD

For breakfast, spread slices of this nutty loaf with honey butter. At noon, team the bread with chicken or ham salad for a first-rate sandwich. Serve it with slices of Swiss cheese for an afternoon snack.

1½-pound (24 servings)	Ingredients	2-pound (36 servings)
⅔ cup	evaporated milk	¾ cup
¼ cup	water	⅓ cup
1	egg(s)	2
¼ cup	margarine or butter, cut up	⅓ cup
3½ cups	bread flour	4⅔ cups
⅓ cup	granulated sugar	½ cup
¾ teaspoon	salt	1 teaspoon
1 teaspoon	active dry yeast or bread machine yeast	1¼ teaspoons
2 cups	ground walnuts	2⅔ cups
⅓ cup	packed brown sugar	½ cup
3 tablespoons	granulated sugar	¼ cup
½ teaspoon	vanilla	¾ teaspoon
⅓ cup	evaporated milk	½ cup
1 tablespoon	margarine or butter, softened	4 teaspoons
1	beaten egg* (optional)	1
1 tablespoon	evaporated milk or milk* (optional)	1 tablespoon

NUTRITION FACTS PER SERVING

		Daily Values
Calories	202	10%
Total fat	10 g	15%
Sat. fat	2 g	8%
Cholesterol	12 mg	3%
Sodium	110 mg	4%
Carbo.	24 g	8%
Fiber	1 g	4%
Protein	5 g	

Select the recipe size. Add the first 8 ingredients to the machine according to the manufacturer's directions. Select the dough cycle. When the cycle is complete, remove dough from machine. Punch down. Divide the 1½-pound dough in half or divide the 2-pound dough into thirds. Cover and let rest for 10 minutes.

Meanwhile, for the filling, in a medium mixing bowl stir together the walnuts, brown sugar, 3 tablespoons or ¼ cup granulated sugar, and the vanilla. Stir in the ⅓ or ½ cup evaporated milk and the softened margarine or butter. (Mixture should be easy to spread. If necessary, stir in a little additional evaporated milk.) Set aside.

For the 1½- or 2-pound recipe, grease baking sheets. Roll each portion of the dough into a 16×10-inch rectangle. Evenly divide filling among rectangles and spread filling evenly to edges. Starting from a long side, loosely roll up each rectangle, jelly-roll style. (If rolled too tightly, the filling may cause the dough to crack during baking.) Moisten edges; pinch to seal.

Place loaves, seams down, on the prepared baking sheets. Prick tops with a fork. Cover and let rise in a warm place for 45 to 60 minutes or until nearly double. If desired, stir together the beaten egg and the 1 tablespoon milk; brush over loaves.

Bake in a 350° oven for 30 to 35 minutes or until bread sounds hollow when lightly tapped. (If necessary to prevent overbrowning, cover loosely with foil the last 20 minutes of baking.) Cool on a wire rack.

*Note: Our Test Kitchen recommends 1 beaten egg and 1 tablespoon evaporated milk or milk for either size recipe.

FRUIT AND NUT CINNAMON ROLLS

To slice the dough for these scrumptious rolls, use this simple trick: Place a length of thread under the roll of dough where you want to make the cut. Bring the ends of the thread up and around the sides of the roll, crisscrossing the thread on top. Pull the ends of the thread quickly, cutting through the dough.

1½-pound (18 rolls)	Ingredients	2-pound (24 rolls)
¾ cup	milk	1 cup
1	egg(s)	2
¼ cup	margarine or butter, cut up	⅓ cup
3 cups	bread flour	4 cups
¼ cup	granulated sugar	⅓ cup
¾ teaspoon	salt	1 teaspoon
1 teaspoon	active dry yeast or bread machine yeast	1¼ teaspoons
½ cup	packed brown sugar	¾ cup
3 tablespoons	bread flour	¼ cup
1½ teaspoons	ground cinnamon	2 teaspoons
⅓ cup	margarine or butter	½ cup
¾ cup	coarsely chopped pecans, toasted	1 cup
¾ cup	mixed dried fruit bits	1 cup
	milk	
	Powdered Sugar Glaze (optional)	

NUTRITION FACTS PER ROLL		
		Daily Values
Calories	225	11%
Total fat	10 g	15%
Sat. fat	2 g	8%
Cholesterol	13 mg	4%
Sodium	173 mg	7%
Carbo.	31 g	10%
Fiber	1 g	4%
Protein	4 g	

Select the recipe size. Add the first 7 ingredients to the machine according to the manufacturer's directions. Select the dough cycle. When the cycle is complete, remove dough from machine. Punch the dough down. Cover and let rest for 10 minutes.

Meanwhile, for filling, combine the brown sugar, 3 tablespoons or ¼ cup flour, and the cinnamon. With pastry blender or fork, cut in the ⅓ or ½ cup margarine or butter until crumbly. Set aside.

For the 1½-pound recipe, grease two 8×1½-inch round baking pans. Sprinkle pecans over the prepared pans. On a lightly floured surface, roll the dough into an 18×8-inch rectangle. Sprinkle filling over dough; sprinkle dried fruit bits over filling. Starting from a long side, roll up, jelly-roll style; seal edge. Cut into eighteen 1-inch-thick slices. Place, cut sides down, in prepared pans. Cover and let rise in a warm place about 45 minutes or until nearly double. Brush with milk. Bake in a 375° oven for 25 to 30 minutes or until rolls sound hollow when lightly tapped. (If necessary to prevent overbrowning, cover rolls loosely with foil the last 5 to 10 minutes of baking.) Loosen edges and immediately invert onto wire racks. Cool slightly. If desired, drizzle with Powdered Sugar Glaze. Serve warm.

For the 2-pound recipe, grease one 13×9×2-inch baking pan and one 8×1½-inch round baking pan. Sprinkle pecans over prepared pans. Divide dough in half. On a lightly floured surface, roll half of the dough into a 12×8-inch rectangle. Sprinkle half of the filling over

rectangle; sprinkle half of the dried fruit bits over filling. Starting from a long side, roll up, jelly-roll style; seal edge. Cut roll into twelve 1-inch-thick slices. Repeat with remaining half of dough, remaining filling, and remaining dried fruit bits. Place slices, cut sides down, in prepared pans (16 in large pan, 8 in smaller pan). Cover and let rise in a warm place about 45 minutes or until nearly double. Brush with milk. Bake in a 375° oven for 25 to 30 minutes or until rolls sound hollow when lightly tapped. (If necessary to prevent overbrowning, cover rolls loosely with foil the last 5 to 10 minutes of baking.) Loosen edges and immediately invert onto wire racks. Cool slightly. If desired, drizzle with Powdered Sugar Glaze. Serve warm.

Powdered Sugar Glaze: In a bowl stir together 1⅓ cups sifted *powdered sugar,* 1 teaspoon *light-colored corn syrup,* and ½ teaspoon *vanilla.* Stir in enough *milk* (1 to 2 tablespoons) to make glaze of drizzling consistency.

RAISIN BUBBLE RING

A kissing cousin to monkey bread, this raisin-studded ring is made from balls of dough coated in sugar and nutmeg. The balls are stacked in a fluted tube pan and baked.

1½-pound (12 servings)	Ingredients	2-pound (16 servings)
⅔ cup	milk	¾ cup
¼ cup	water	⅓ cup
1	egg*	1
¼ cup	margarine or butter, cut up	⅓ cup
3 cups	bread flour	4 cups
3 tablespoons	sugar	¼ cup
1½ teaspoons	finely shredded orange peel	2 teaspoons
¾ teaspoon	salt	1 teaspoon
¼ teaspoon	ground nutmeg	½ teaspoon
1½ teaspoons	active dry yeast or bread machine yeast	2 teaspoons
¾ cup	dark raisins	1 cup
½ cup	sugar	⅔ cup
¼ teaspoon	ground nutmeg	½ teaspoon
3 tablespoons	margarine or butter, melted	¼ cup

NUTRITION FACTS
PER SERVING

		Daily Values
Calories	270	13%
Total fat	8 g	12%
Sat. fat	2 g	8%
Cholesterol	19 mg	6%
Sodium	225 mg	9%
Carbo.	45 g	14%
Fiber	2 g	6%
Protein	6 g	

Select the recipe size. Add the first 11 ingredients to the machine according to the manufacturer's directions. Select the dough cycle. When the cycle is complete, remove dough from machine. Punch down. Cover and let rest for 10 minutes.

For the 1½-pound recipe, grease a 10-inch fluted tube pan. Divide dough into 24 balls. In a small mixing bowl stir together the ½ cup sugar and ¼ teaspoon nutmeg. Dip each ball into the melted margarine or butter, then roll it in the sugar-nutmeg mixture. Arrange half of the coated balls of dough in the bottom of the prepared pan. Make a second layer, positioning the balls of dough between the balls of dough in the lower layer. Drizzle any remaining melted margarine or butter and sprinkle any remaining sugar-nutmeg mixture over balls. Cover; let rise in a warm place about 30 minutes or until nearly double. Bake in a 325° oven 35 to 40 minutes or until bread sounds hollow when lightly tapped. (If necessary to prevent overbrowning, cover with foil the last 10 minutes of baking.) Cool 1 minute on a wire rack. Invert onto a serving plate; remove pan. Serve warm.

For the 2-pound recipe, grease a 10-inch fluted tube pan. Divide dough into 32 balls. In a small mixing bowl stir together the ⅔ cup sugar and ½ teaspoon nutmeg. Dip each ball into the melted margarine or butter, then roll it in the sugar-nutmeg mixture. Arrange about one-third of the coated balls of dough in the bottom of the prepared pan. Make a second and third layer, positioning the balls of dough between the balls of dough in the next lower layer. Drizzle any remaining melted margarine or butter and sprinkle any remaining sugar-nutmeg mixture over balls. Cover; let rise in a warm place about 30 minutes or until nearly double. Bake in a 325° oven 35 to 40 minutes or until bread sounds hollow when lightly tapped. (If necessary to prevent overbrowning, cover with foil the last 10 minutes of baking.) Cool 1 minute on a wire rack. Invert onto a serving plate; remove pan. Serve warm.

*Note: Our Test Kitchen recommends 1 egg for either size recipe.

ALMOND BRUNCH LOAF

For an elegant brunch, serve this simple but impressive coffee cake with cheesy scrambled eggs, slices of Canadian-style bacon, and a selection of fruit juices.

1½-pound (12 servings)	Ingredients	2-pound (16 servings)
⅔ cup	milk	¾ cup
1	egg*	1
2 tablespoons	margarine or butter, cut up	3 tablespoons
3 cups	bread flour	4 cups
1 tablespoon	sugar	4 teaspoons
¾ teaspoon	salt	1 teaspoon
1 teaspoon	finely shredded orange peel	1¼ teaspoons
1¼ teaspoons	active dry yeast or bread machine yeast	1½ teaspoons
1 cup	ground almonds	1¼ cups
¼ cup	sugar	⅓ cup
½ teaspoon	finely shredded orange peel	¾ teaspoon
3 tablespoons	orange juice	¼ cup
	orange juice	
	sugar	

NUTRITION FACTS PER SERVING

		Daily Values
Calories	229	11%
Total fat	8 g	11%
Sat. fat	1 g	5%
Cholesterol	19 mg	6%
Sodium	168 mg	7%
Carbo.	33 g	11%
Fiber	2 g	7%
Protein	8 g	

Select the recipe size. Add the first 8 ingredients to the machine according to the manufacturer's directions. Select the dough cycle. When the cycle is complete, remove dough from machine. Punch down. Cover and let rest for 10 minutes.

Meanwhile, for the filling, in a small mixing bowl stir together the ground almonds, 1/4 or 1/3 cup sugar, 1/2 or 3/4 teaspoon orange peel, and 3 tablespoons or 1/4 cup orange juice. (If filling is not easy to spread, stir in additional orange juice.)

Lightly grease a baking sheet. On a lightly floured surface, roll the 1 1/2-pound dough into a 24×10-inch rectangle. (For the 2-pound recipe, roll dough into a 24×12-inch rectangle.) Spread the filling over dough rectangle to within 1/2 inch of the edges. Fold dough loosely from a short side, making seven 3-inch-wide folds. (This is similar to rolling

a jelly roll, except you fold the dough instead of rolling it.) Transfer to the prepared baking sheet. On each of the long sides, make 1-inch-long cuts from the edges toward the center at about 1-inch intervals. Cover; let rise in a warm place about 30 minutes or until nearly double.

Bake in a 350° oven for 35 to 40 minutes or until bread sounds hollow when lightly tapped. (If necessary to prevent overbrowning, cover loosely with foil the last 5 to 10 minutes of baking.) Lightly brush with orange juice; sprinkle with sugar. Serve warm.

*Note: Our Test Kitchen recommends 1 egg for either size recipe.

LATTICE COFFEE CAKE

If you don't want to take the time to weave the strips of dough over and under each other, arrange the number of strips you want to run lengthwise in the pan, then top with the remaining strips going in the opposite direction, forming a basket-weave pattern.

1½-pound (12 servings)	Ingredients	2-pound (16 servings)
¾ cup	milk	1 cup
2	beaten egg yolks	3
2 tablespoons	margarine or butter, cut up	3 tablespoons
3 cups	bread flour	4 cups
¼ cup	packed brown sugar	⅓ cup
¾ teaspoon	salt	1 teaspoon
½ teaspoon	ground mace	¾ teaspoon
1½ teaspoons	active dry yeast or bread machine yeast	2 teaspoons
⅓ cup	apricot, pineapple, or strawberry preserves	½ cup
3 tablespoons	margarine or butter, softened	¼ cup
¼ cup	chopped almonds	⅓ cup

NUTRITION FACTS PER SERVING		
		Daily Values
Calories	236	11%
Total fat	8 g	11%
Sat. fat	2 g	7%
Cholesterol	37 mg	12%
Sodium	201 mg	8%
Carbo.	36 g	12%
Fiber	1 g	5%
Protein	6 g	

Select the recipe size. Add the first 8 ingredients to the machine according to the manufacturer's directions. Select the dough cycle. When the cycle is complete, remove dough from machine. Punch dough down; cover and let rest 10 minutes.

For the the 1½-pound recipe, grease an 11×7×1½-inch baking pan; pat two-thirds of dough into pan. (For the 2-pound recipe, grease a 13×9×2-inch baking pan; pat two-thirds of dough into pan.) Combine preserves, softened margarine or butter, and almonds; spread over

dough. On lightly floured surface, roll the remaining dough into an 11×6-inch rectangle for 1½-pound recipe and a 13×7-inch rectangle for 2-pound recipe. Cut lengthwise into ½-inch wide strips (12 strips for the 1½-pound recipe or 14 strips for the 2-pound recipe). Weave strips in a lattice pattern over filling. Trim excess dough from strips. Cover and let rise in warm place about 1 hour or until nearly double. Bake in a 375° oven for 20 to 25 minutes. (If necessary to prevent overbrowning, cover with foil the last 10 minutes of baking.) Serve warm.

INDEX

METRIC COOKING HINTS

By making a few conversions, cooks in Australia, Canada, and the United Kingdom can use the recipes in *Better Homes and Gardens® Best Bread Machine Recipes* with confidence. The charts on this page provide a guide for converting measurements from the U.S. customary system, which is used throughout this book, to the imperial and metric systems. There also is a conversion table for oven temperatures to accommodate the differences in oven calibrations.

Product Differences: Most of the ingredients called for in the recipes in this book are available in English-speaking countries. However, some are known by different names. Here are some common American ingredients and their possible counterparts:
- Sugar is granulated or castor sugar.
- Powdered sugar is icing sugar.
- All-purpose flour is plain household flour or white flour. When self-rising flour is used in place of all-purpose flour in a recipe that calls for leavening, omit the leavening agent (baking soda or baking powder) and salt.
- Light-colored corn syrup is golden syrup.
- Cornstarch is cornflour.
- Baking soda is bicarbonate of soda.
- Vanilla is vanilla essence.
- Green, red, or yellow sweet peppers are capsicums.
- Golden raisins are sultanas.

Volume and Weight: Americans traditionally use cup measures for liquid and solid ingredients. The chart, below, shows the approximate imperial and metric equivalents. If you are accustomed to weighing solid ingredients, the following approximate equivalents will be helpful.
- 1 cup butter, castor sugar, or rice = 8 ounces = about 250 grams
- 1 cup flour = 4 ounces = about 125 grams
- 1 cup icing sugar = 5 ounces = about 150 grams

Spoon measures are used for smaller amounts of ingredients. Although the size of the tablespoon varies slightly in different countries, for practical purposes and for recipes in this book, a straight substitution is all that's necessary.

Measurements made using cups or spoons always should be level unless stated otherwise.

EQUIVALENTS: U.S. = AUSTRALIA/U.K.

$\frac{1}{8}$ teaspoon = 0.5 ml
$\frac{1}{4}$ teaspoon = 1 ml
$\frac{1}{2}$ teaspoon = 2 ml
1 teaspoon = 5 ml
1 tablespoon = 1 tablespoon
$\frac{1}{4}$ cup = 2 tablespoons = 2 fluid ounces = 60 ml
$\frac{1}{3}$ cup = $\frac{1}{4}$ cup = 3 fluid ounces = 90 ml
$\frac{1}{2}$ cup = $\frac{1}{3}$ cup = 4 fluid ounces = 120 ml
$\frac{2}{3}$ cup = $\frac{1}{2}$ cup = 5 fluid ounces = 150 ml
$\frac{3}{4}$ cup = $\frac{2}{3}$ cup = 6 fluid ounces = 180 ml
1 cup = $\frac{3}{4}$ cup = 8 fluid ounces = 240 ml
$1\frac{1}{4}$ cups = 1 cup
2 cups = 1 pint
1 quart = 1 litre
$\frac{1}{2}$ inch =1.27 cm
1 inch = 2.54 cm

BAKING PAN SIZES

American	Metric
8×1½-inch round baking pan	20×4-centimetre cake tin
9×1½-inch round baking pan	23×3.5-centimetre cake tin
11×7×1½-inch baking pan	28×18×4-centimetre baking tin
13×9×2-inch baking pan	30×20×3-centimetre baking tin
2-quart rectangular baking dish	30×20×3-centimetre baking tin
15×10×1-inch baking pan	30×25×2-centimetre baking tin (Swiss roll tin)
9-inch pie plate	22×4- or 23×4-centimetre pie plate
7- or 8-inch springform pan	18- or 20-centimetre springform or loose-bottom cake tin
9×5×3-inch loaf pan	23×13×7-centimetre or 2-pound narrow loaf tin or paté tin
1½-quart casserole	1.5-litre casserole
2-quart casserole	2-litre casserole

OVEN TEMPERATURE EQUIVALENTS

Fahrenheit Setting	Celsius Setting*	Gas Setting
300°F	150°C	Gas Mark 2 (slow)
325°F	160°C	Gas Mark 3 (moderately slow)
350°F	180°C	Gas Mark 4 (moderate)
375°F	190°C	Gas Mark 5 (moderately hot)
400°F	200°C	Gas Mark 6 (hot)
425°F	220°C	Gas Mark 7
450°F	230°C	Gas Mark 8 (very hot)
Broil		Grill

* Electric and gas ovens may be calibrated using Celsius. However, for an electric oven, increase the Celsius setting 10 to 20 degrees when cooking above 160°C. For convection or forced-air ovens (gas or electric), lower the temperature setting 10°C when cooking at all heat levels.